Space Science

WHAT SATELLITES SEE

How to use this book

Welcome to *Space Science*. All the books in this set are organized to help you through the multitude of pictures and facts that make this subject so interesting. There is also a master glossary for the set on pages 58–64 and an index on pages 65–72.

The text is organized into chapters.

Capitals show key glossary terms. They are defined in the quick reference glossary.

Links to related information in other titles in the *Space Science* set.

Chapter heading.

Photographs and diagrams have been carefully selected and annotated for clarity. Captions provide more facts.

Quick reference glossary. All these glossary entries, sometimes with further explanation, appear in the master glossary for the set on pages 58–64.

First published in 2004 by
Atlantic Europe Publishing Company Ltd.

Author
Brian Knapp, BSc, PhD

Art Director
Duncan McCrae, BSc

Senior Designer
Adele Humphries, BA, PGCE

Editors
Mary Sanders, BSc, and Gillian Gatehouse

Illustrations on behalf of Earthscape Editions
David Woodroffe and David Hardy

Design and production
EARTHSCAPE EDITIONS

Print
WKT Company Limited, Hong Kong

This product is manufactured from sustainable managed forests. For every tree cut down, at least one more is planted.

***Space science* – Volume 8: What satellites see**
A CIP record for this book is available from the British Library

ISBN 1 86214 370 6

Picture credits
All photographs and diagrams NASA except the following:
(c=center t=top b=bottom l=left r=right)

Earthscape Editions 7, 9b, 14b, 15, 45t, 48–49t, 49c, 49b, 57; *used with permission of Lucent Technologies Inc./Bell Labs* 8t; *NOAA* 24tl, 24cl, 24bl, 25tr, 25br; *Space Imaging* 17.

The front cover shows a satellite view of water vapor in the air; the back cover, the Hubble Space Telescope.

NASA, the U.S. National Aeronautics and Space Administration, was founded in 1958 for aeronautical and space exploration. It operates several installations around the country and has its headquarters in Washington, D.C.

CONTENTS

▶ The world at night.

1: WHAT SATELLITES CAN DO

If you were to ask people about the progress we have made in **SPACE**, many would almost certainly think of the **SPACE SHUTTLE**, journeys to the **MOON**, and **PROBES** sent to the edges of the **SOLAR SYSTEM**. They might not think as quickly of the news broadcast they have just watched or the telephone call they last made, or tomorrow's weather. But each of these areas is of more day-to-day importance to people than the glamorous trips to the Moon.

In fact, there are two sides to space science: the glamorous side and the workaday side. The glamorous side includes missions to the Moon, to Mars, and beyond. These missions provide fascinating insights into our **UNIVERSE**. The technology used in space science has also been truly beneficial for designing things in the world around us. But it is the workaday side dominated by just one thing—the **SATELLITE**—that pays the space science wages of many.

A satellite is anything that is in **ORBIT** around a **CELESTIAL** body. The Moon, for example, is a natural satellite of the Earth. The Earth is a satellite of the **SUN**.

Most man-made satellites are in orbit around the Earth, but there are also satellites in orbit around the Sun and other planets. The **INTERNATIONAL SPACE STATION** is an Earth satellite. Even the Space Shuttle is a satellite when it is not in takeoff or reentry mode.

Simple tasks done well

Apart from the last two examples, a satellite does not carry people, it does not do a range of jobs, and it is not glamorous. Usually, a satellite does just one job. The fact that most satellites are for a single purpose is shown in their names: communications satellite, weather satellite, **GLOBAL POSITIONING SYSTEM** (GPS) satellite, and so on.

For more on the Shuttle and International Space Station see Volume 7: *Shuttle to Space Station*.

▶ Although each satellite performs a "simple" task, it is possible to combine images obtained by several satellites. Here is an example using the information from four satellites, which helps show how various natural patterns over the Earth are interrelated. The images used were: land; vegetation; fire (red); windblown dust (colored patterns over the oceans); and clouds.

CELESTIAL Relating to the sky above, the "heavens."

GLOBAL POSITIONING SYSTEM A network of geostationary satellites that can be used to locate the position of any object on the Earth's surface.

INTERNATIONAL SPACE STATION The international orbiting space laboratory.

MOON The natural satellite that orbits the Earth.

ORBIT The path followed by one object as it tracks around another.

PROBE An unmanned spacecraft designed to explore our solar system and beyond.

SATELLITE A man-made object that orbits the Earth.

SOLAR SYSTEM The Sun and the bodies orbiting around it.

SPACE Everything beyond the Earth's atmosphere.

SPACE SHUTTLE NASA's reusable space vehicle that is launched like a rocket but returns like a glider.

SUN The star that the planets of the solar system revolve around.

UNIVERSE The entirety of everything there is; the cosmos.

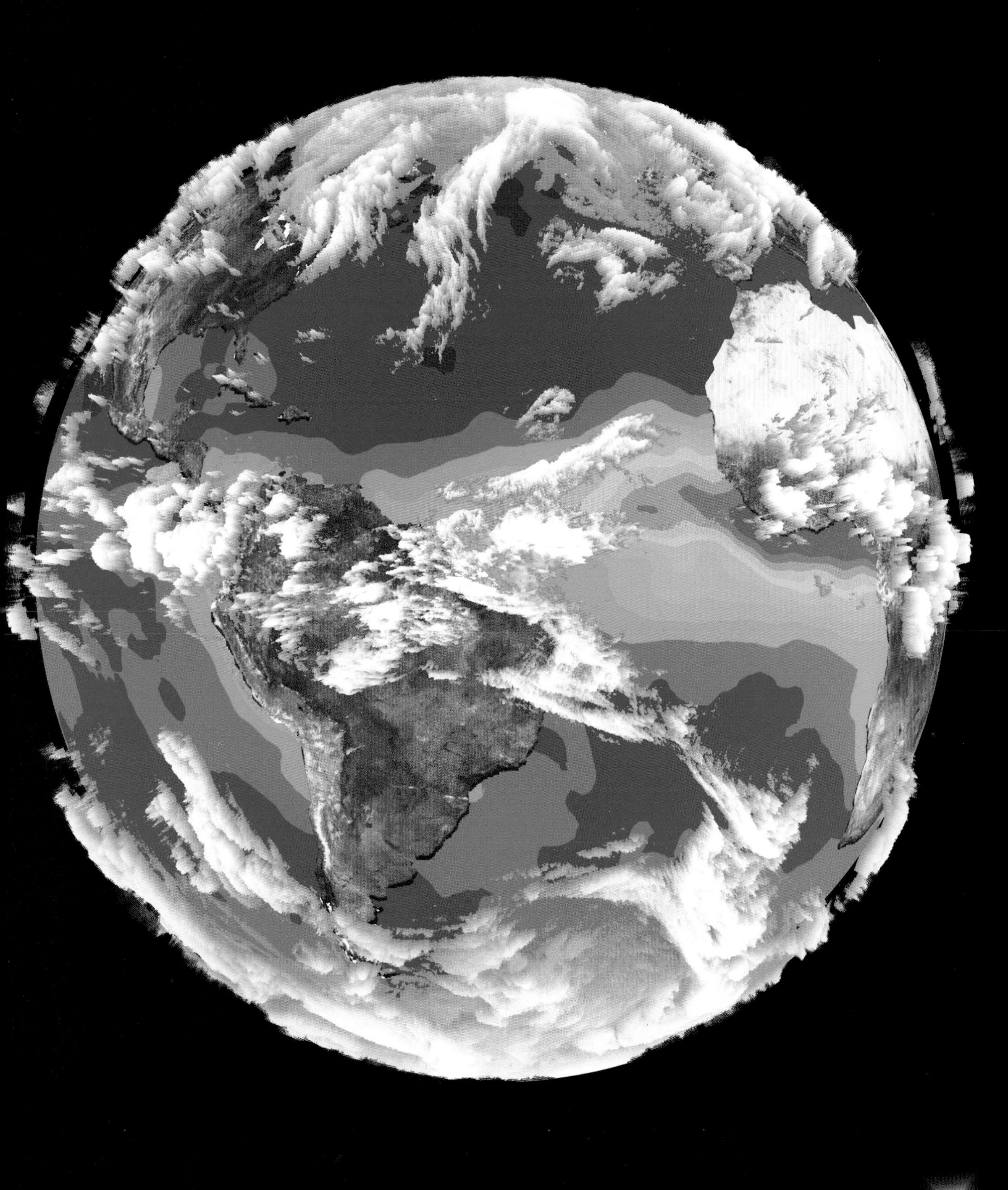

But that has the advantage that a satellite's design can be honed for its single task without the compromises that are needed for a multitask machine. So, what each satellite does, it does well, and as a result, many satellites are extremely reliable and profitable.

Wide area coverage

Think about the way a satellite works, and you can immediately see some of its advantages. First and foremost, it is a wireless connection, so it can be reached as successfully from the Amazon rain forest as from an office in the financial district of Wall Street, New York, or while you are walking to school.

Placed in orbit, it can "look down" on a large sector of the globe, so a fairly small number of satellites can provide global coverage.

More money probably went into satellites from the very beginning of space exploration than into Moon missions. But for a long time the purposes and even the existence of many of the satellites were clouded in secrecy because they were for military missions, which in reality means they were used to spy on other countries. Today, quite separate military satellite systems still orbit in the skies, taking pictures, forwarding communications, and listening in on other networks.

Paying for a satellite

Because the military has lots of money, some things were swiftly created that might never otherwise have been developed. The research teams in the companies that made the military satellites could then use some of the principles they had learned for other purposes.

What was important was to cover the cost of manufacture, launch, and survival of a nonmilitary satellite. Launching even a small **PAYLOAD** requires a large **ROCKET** to get it there and costs tens of billions of dollars.

For more on the development of rockets and satellites see Volume 6: *Journey into space*.

In general, there are two ways to pay for such satellite launches: They can be financed by the government and the information made available for research (**NASA** and **ESA** satellites are examples), or they can be used for a commercial purpose because ordinary people will pay for their use (as is the case with television and telephone links and **GLOBAL POSITIONING SYSTEMS**).

▼ This diagram shows how three **GEOSTATIONARY SATELLITES** in orbit around the **EQUATOR** can communicate to all of the globe except areas close to the **POLES**. **UPLINKS** and **DOWNLINKS** can be made within each shaded zone.

Each satellite has a direct line of sight over an area with a diameter of 18,000 km centered on the equator. The Earth's diameter is 21,000 km, so only a small area at each pole is not covered. Links across the world are made by uplinking to a satellite, which then links to one of the other satellites. The signal is then downlinked from that satellite to the destination.

DOWNLINK A communication to Earth from a spacecraft.

EQUATOR The ring drawn around a body midway between the poles.

ESA The European Space Agency.

GEOSTATIONARY SATELLITE A man-made satellite in a fixed or geosynchronous orbit around the Earth.

GLOBAL POSITIONING SYSTEM A network of geostationary satellites that can be used to locate the position of any object on the Earth's surface.

NASA The National Aeronautics and Space Administration.

PAYLOAD The spacecraft that is carried into space by a launcher.

POLE The geographic pole is the place where a line drawn along the axis of rotation exits from a body's surface.

ROCKET Any kind of device that uses the principle of jet propulsion, that is, the rapid release of gases designed to propel an object rapidly.

UPLINK A communication from Earth to a spacecraft.

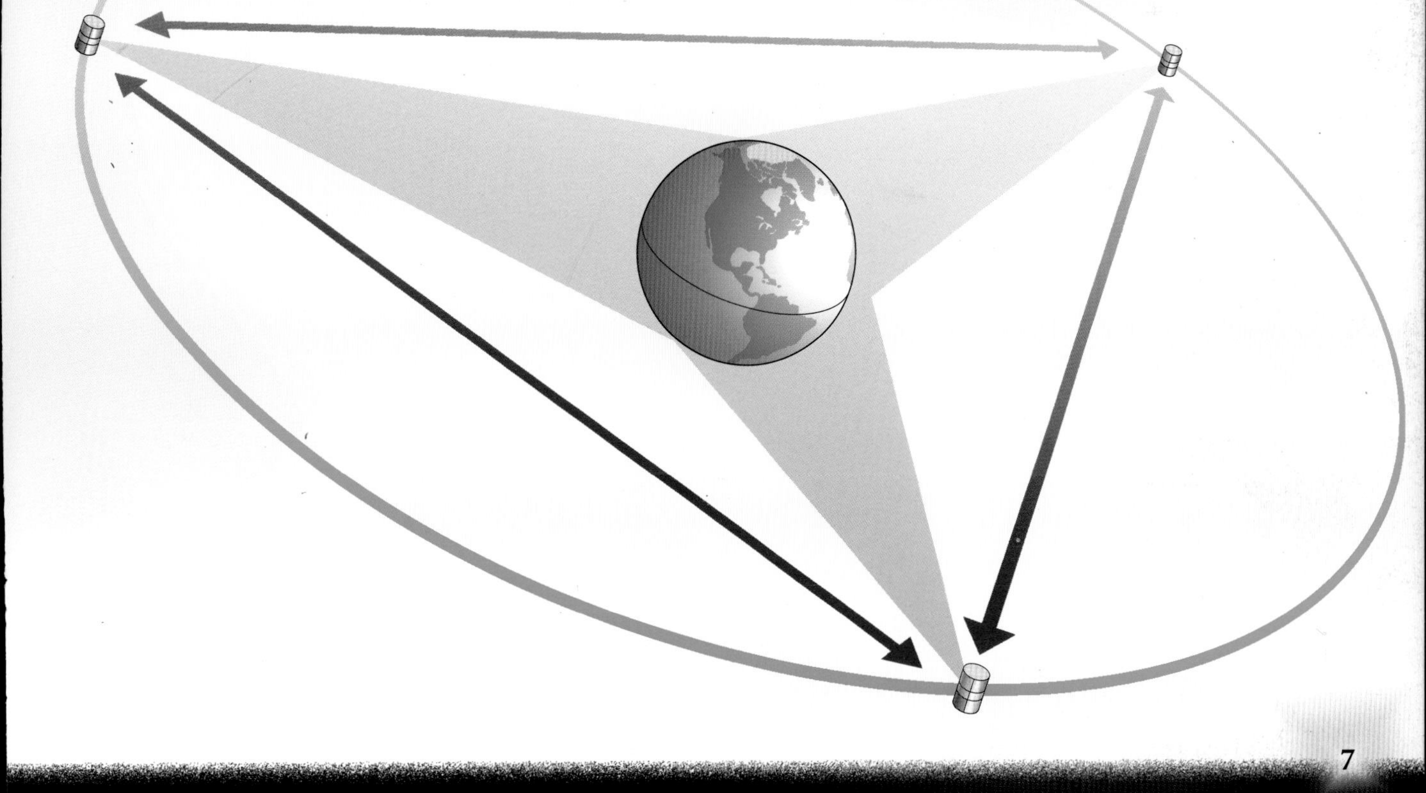

▶ The first commercial communications satellite was Telstar.

The scope of satellites

What satellites do depends on the **SENSOR** installed. While we might think of them as relaying telephone calls or taking pictures of the Earth, what they can do is, in reality, far more than that. For example, satellites can sense wavelengths of **RADIATION** that we cannot see (for example, **INFRARED** and heat) and hence send back information that was previously unavailable to us.

Satellites can look up as well as down. If they look up, they see space. And since they are unaffected by the absorbing effects of the Earth's **ATMOSPHERE**, they can tell us more about the universe we live in than we could possibly know just from the planet's surface.

The first satellites

Although the early satellites were mostly military, the world's first satellite was a very public affair.

The satellite era began on October 4, 1957, when the world's first satellite, Sputnik 1, was launched by the then Soviet Union. This satellite, a 58-cm shiny ball, simply sent out a series of bleeps. But the bleeps varied in **FREQUENCY** with the temperature of the satellite, so in that sense, even the first satellite sent back details of what it could "see." Sputnik transmitted in the short-wave band, and so it was equipped with whip **ANTENNAE**, not with the microwave dishes used today.

But what it mainly demonstrated was that a satellite could be very simple. Modern satellites are not simple. Sputnik's simplicity and performance gave a lot of confidence to those who made satellites in later years and to those who paid for them.

▼ The first satellites were mainly **REFLECTING** satellites. Explorer 24, shown here, was a 4-meter diameter inflatable sphere (ball-shaped). It provided information on relationships between **SOLAR RADIATION** and **DENSITY** in the air.

Echo, another inflatable made of a plastic called mylar, was 30 meters in diameter. Once in orbit, air inside the balloon expanded, and the balloon began its task of reflecting radio transmissions from one **GROUND STATION** back to another. Echo 1 satellites generated a lot of interest because, as they orbited, they could be seen with the naked eye.

▲ The world's first satellite, Sputnik, was of very simple construction, since Russian scientists were most interested in making sure they could successfully put an object into orbit rather than worrying about the nature of the satellite. It would not take long for more sophisticated satellites to follow.

ANTENNA (pl. **ANTENNAE**) A device, often in the shape of a rod or wire, used for sending out and receiving radio waves.

ATMOSPHERE The envelope of gases that surrounds the Earth and other bodies in the universe.

DENSITY A measure of the amount of matter in a space.

FREQUENCY The number of complete cycles of (for example, radio) waves received per second.

GROUND STATION A receiving and transmitting station in direct communication with satellites. Such stations are characterized by having large dish-shaped antennae.

INFRARED Radiation with a wavelength that is longer than red light.

RADIATION The transfer of energy in the form of waves (such as light and heat) or particles (such as from radioactive decay of a material).

REFLECT To bounce back any light that falls on a surface.

SENSOR A device used to detect something.

SOLAR RADIATION The light and heat energy sent into space from the Sun.

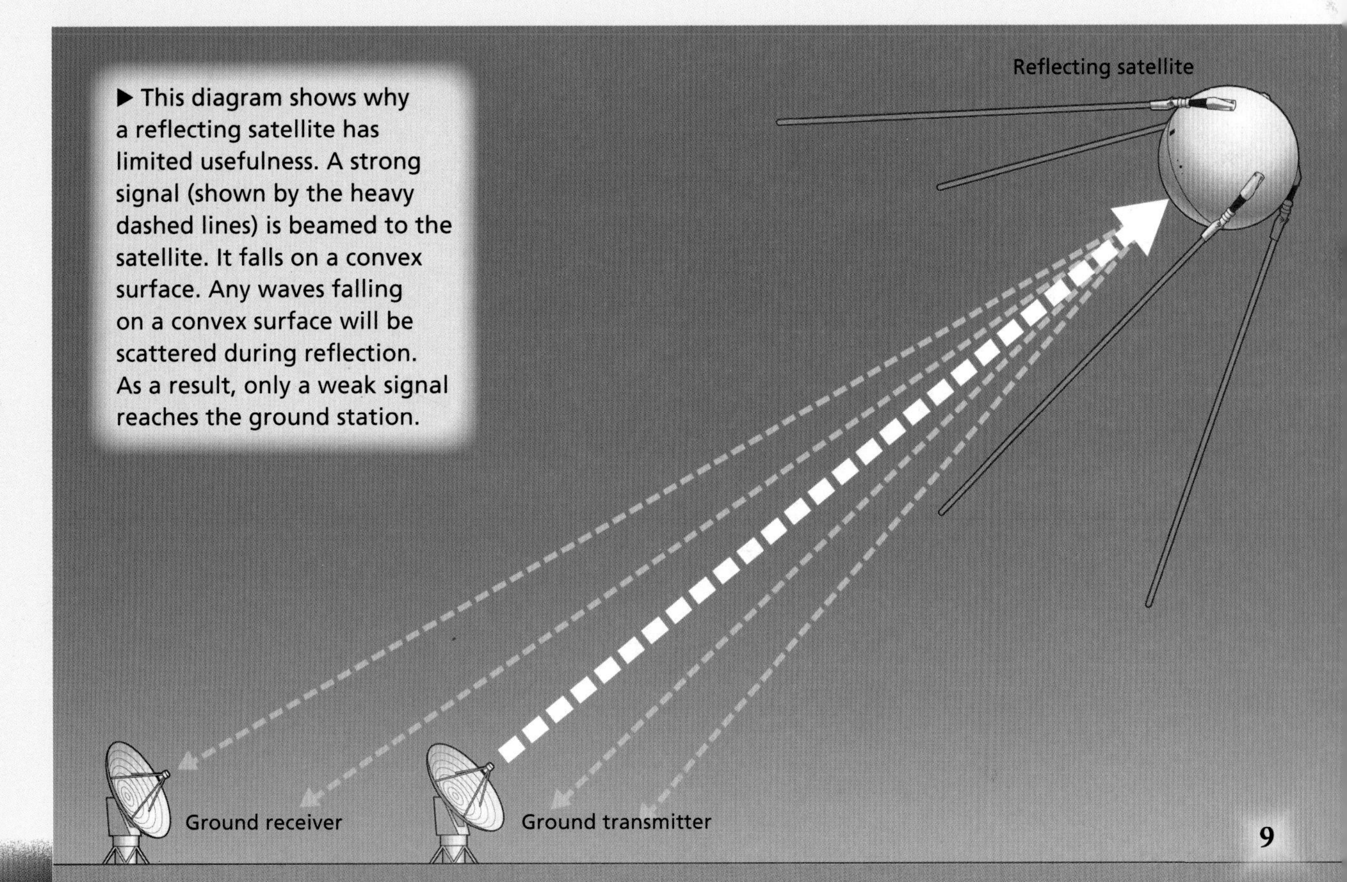

▶ This diagram shows why a reflecting satellite has limited usefulness. A strong signal (shown by the heavy dashed lines) is beamed to the satellite. It falls on a convex surface. Any waves falling on a convex surface will be scattered during reflection. As a result, only a weak signal reaches the ground station.

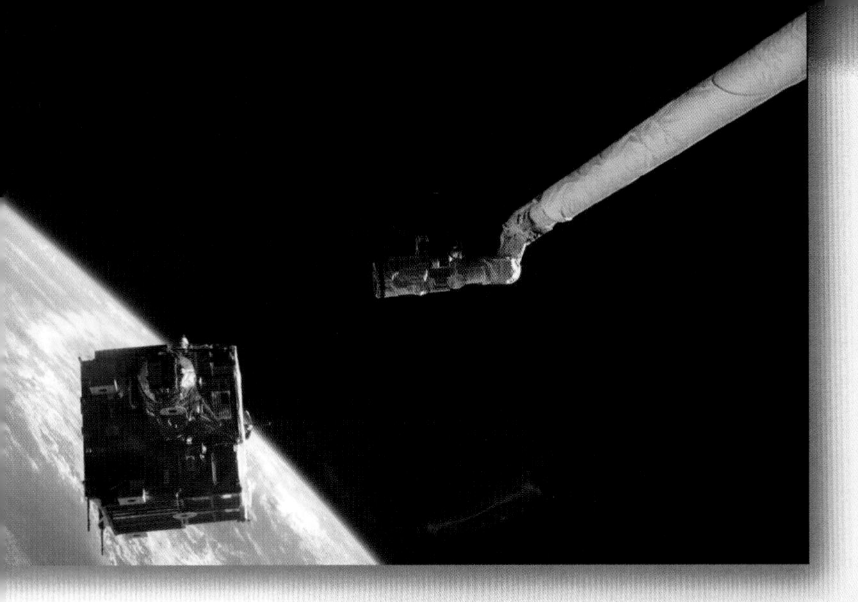

◀ A satellite being released from a Space Shuttle using its remote manipulator system.

Launching a satellite

Satellites can be put in orbit directly from a **LAUNCHER** (as the European Space Agency does using an Ariane rocket fired from French Guiana), or they can be released from the Space Shuttle, as many American satellites are.

Whether the satellite is put in orbit from a **ROCKET** or from the Space Shuttle, the launching is just the same. A set of powerful motors lifts the whole rocket off the ground and vertically upward through the thickest part of the atmosphere. This saves fuel.

At about 200 km from the ground the launcher motors are reprogrammed to angle the rocket eastward. This is the same direction as the Earth rotates in, and so the rocket is given a free boost. Launching from the equator gives the maximum boost, so most launch sites are as close to the equator as national boundaries allow (NASA is in Florida, for example).

At this point an inertial guidance system (IGS) puts the payload satellite into exactly the right orbit. In the correct orbit the **GRAVITATIONAL PULL** on the satellite from the Earth is exactly balanced by the **CENTRIFUGAL FORCE** from the movement of the satellite.

For more on launching rockets see Volume 6: *Journey into space*.

Satellite servicing by Space Shuttle

▶ Satellites can be launched from the Space Shuttle, which has a cargo bay big enough to carry several satellites in a single mission. This pays for the extra cost of using the Shuttle. However, the Space Shuttle can also be used to send up a repair crew when a satellite has problems.

A typical satellite might take 4 years to make. It might cost a further $100 million to launch one into orbit. But if something goes wrong, it may cost another $100 million to send a Space Shuttle up to repair it and maybe put it into a new orbit. Although nothing is saved in direct costs compared with building a new satellite, an awful lot is saved in time (and thus profitable operation at perhaps $100 million a year) by having the satellite repaired.

This picture shows three crew members of Space Shuttle mission STS-49 manipulating the 4.5-tonne satellite INTELSAT VI into the payload bay.

CENTRIFUGAL FORCE A force that acts on an orbiting or spinning body, tending to oppose gravity and move away from the center of rotation.

GRAVITATIONAL PULL The force of attraction between bodies. The larger an object, the more its gravitational pull on other objects.

LAUNCHER A system of propellant tanks and rocket motors or engines designed to lift a payload into space. It may, or may not, be part of a space vehicle.

ROCKET Any kind of device that uses the principle of jet propulsion, that is, the rapid release of gases designed to propel an object rapidly.

NASA
HUGHES

ITED STATES

Orbiting velocity

The **VELOCITY** the rocket has to reach to put the satellite into this position varies, depending on the altitude that the satellite will have for its final orbit. The closer the satellite is to the Earth, the more powerful the **GRAVITY** and the faster the satellite must move in order to stay in orbit.

The velocity it must maintain over and above the **ROTATION** of the Earth is about 27,000 km/hr at 250 km altitude, 11,000 km/hr at 36,000 km altitude, and so on. Satellites moving in these low orbits gain speed on the Earth, and so they see all of the surface. These are very useful orbits for satellites surveying the surface.

Many surveying satellites with cameras are put into a polar orbit at a low altitude of between 500 and 1,000 km. In this way the satellite's orbit remains fixed in space, and the whole Earth rotates below it.

Other science satellites usually orbit higher, perhaps at 5,000 to 10,000 km altitude.

GLOBAL POSITIONING SYSTEM (GPS) satellites are not in **GEOSYNCHRONOUS ORBITS**, but actually sweep across the Earth (they are in **ASYNCHRONOUS** orbits). They are mainly at an altitude 15,000 to 20,000 km.

When it reaches a height of 35,786 km, the satellite does not need to gain on the Earth at all in order to stay in orbit. This is known as a **GEOSTATIONARY ORBIT**, and it is one of the most useful orbits of all for such things as communications. The fact that you can use a simple stationary satellite dish that always points the same way on your home, rather than having to have one that continually tracks satellites across the sky, is thanks to the geosynchronous orbit of the satellite nearest you.

When a rocket or a shuttle releases a satellite, the orbit that the satellite originally takes is rarely truly circular because the release mechanism is fairly crude. Satellites have to have small motors on board so that ground control teams can make the necessary corrections.

◀ Nimbus E, the sixth spacecraft in the Nimbus series, is shown preparing for launch in 1972 by the thrust-augmented Delta vehicle. The satellite was placed in an 1,100-kilometer polar orbit.

ASYNCHRONOUS Not connected in time or pace.

GEOSTATIONARY ORBIT A circular orbit 35,786 km directly above the Earth's equator.

GEOSYNCHRONOUS ORBIT An orbit in which a satellite makes one circuit of the Earth in 24 hours.

GLOBAL POSITIONING SYSTEM A network of geostationary satellites that can be used to locate the position of any object on the Earth's surface.

GRAVITY The force of attraction between bodies.

ROTATION Spinning around an axis.

VELOCITY A more precise word to describe how something is moving, because movement has both a magnitude (speed) and a direction.

Formation satellites

As you read through the preceding pages, you will have seen how satellites were planned one at a time. The only exceptions to this were the **GEOSTATIONARY SATELLITES** in **GEOSYNCHRONOUS ORBIT** intended to provide global communications coverage, the global weather satellites, and the Landsat series (see pages 34–39) for surveying the Earth's surface.

The advantage of having many satellites linked and operational at the same time is that it is possible to find out what is going on across the entire globe in real time. There is no longer any need to wait until the next pass of a single satellite. You can see how important this would be for weather forecasting, for example.

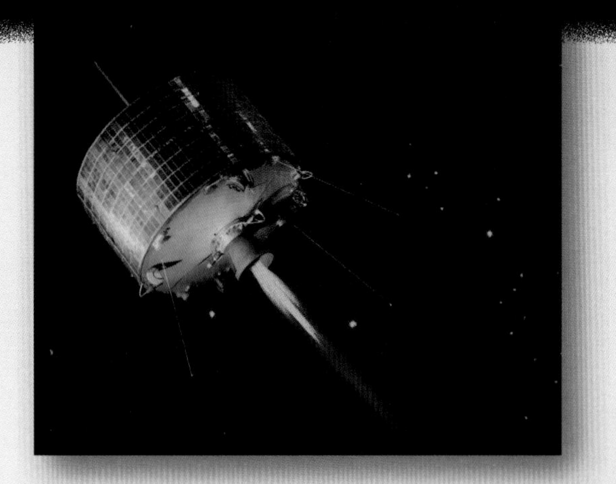

▲ This is Syncom, the first geostationary satellite, placed in orbit 35,786 km from Earth. It transmitted live coverage of the Olympic Games in Tokyo in 1964 to stations in North America and Europe. It has now been replaced by many more modern satellites. Notice the structure of the satellite, with its **SOLAR PANELS** situated around its sides. A small **ROCKET ENGINE** was used to provide course corrections.

Geosynchronous formations

The earliest example of formation flying is the **GLOBAL POSITIONING SYSTEM** (**GPS**), typified by the satellites called Navstar. There are 27 operational Navstar satellites (24 in use; three others as "spares" to be used as individuals fail). They all have a radio **TRANSPONDER**, which communicates with receivers distributed worldwide and is controlled by parent **GROUND STATIONS.** Their orbits are chosen to be regularly spaced around the Earth. This type of formation flying is known as constellation flying.

The new Terra and Aqua satellites are part of a planned pattern of formation flying. Terra is in formation with Landsat-7 and others. Aqua, which follows Terra about 3 hours later in the same orbit, will eventually be joined by even more satellites in formation.

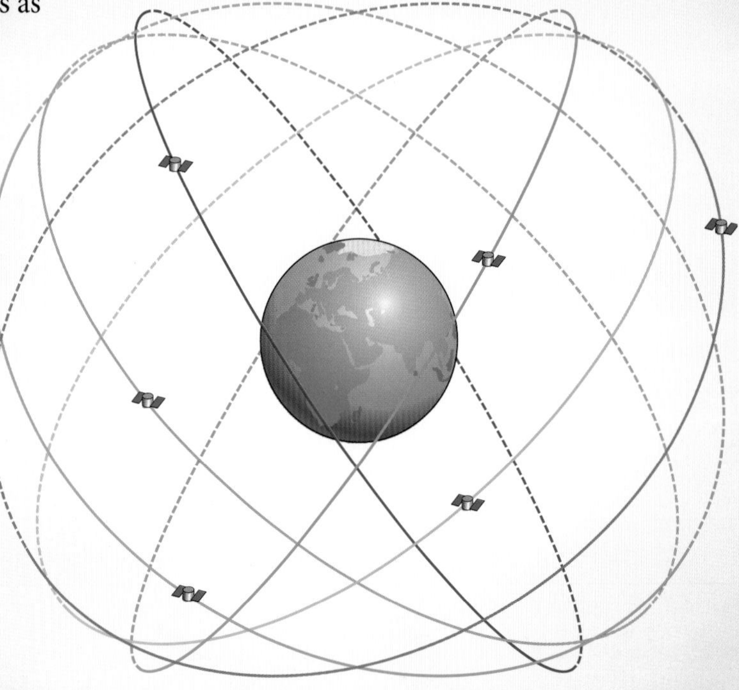

▲ The Navstar pattern of formation flying.

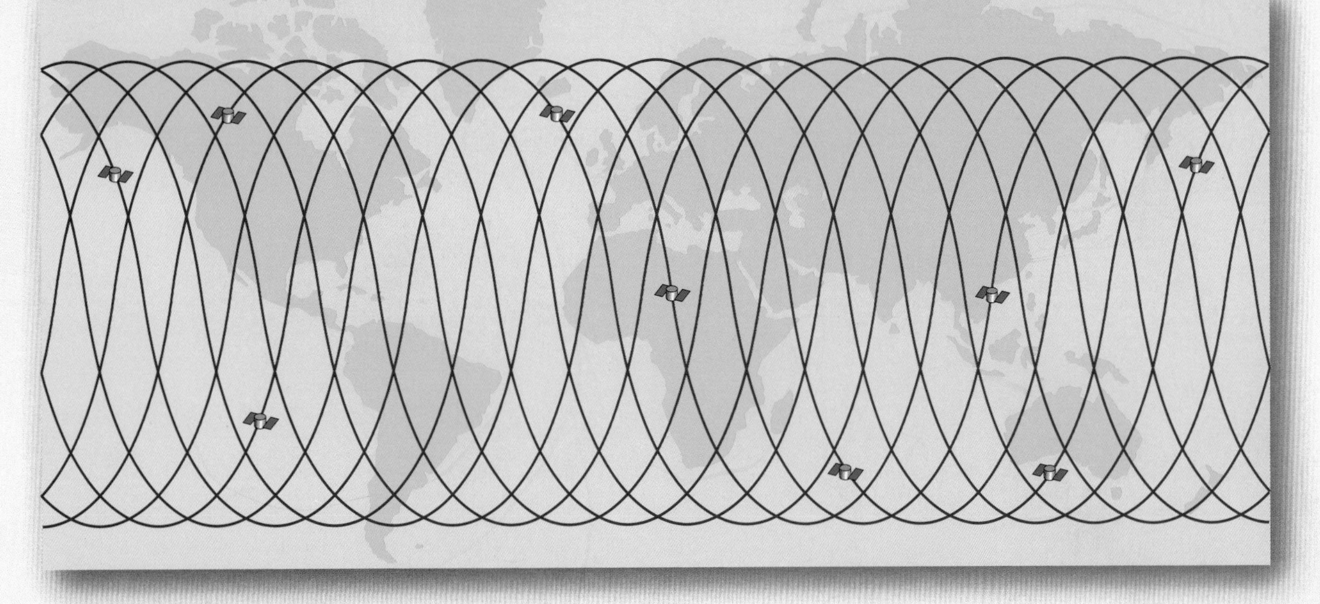

▲ How the Navstar satellites cover the globe.

Terra's orbit around the Earth is timed so that it passes from north to south across the equator in the morning, while Aqua passes south to north over the equator in the afternoon. Terra and Aqua are viewing the entire Earth's surface every 1 to 2 days, acquiring data in 36 spectral bands, or groups, of wavelengths.

By placing satellites close together, each can have its own range of **SENSORS**. But they are effectively sensing at the same time, so they are equivalent to one giant satellite without the problems such a complex satellite might bring in terms of reliability. Furthermore, as more advanced sensors are developed to investigate new things about the Earth, they can be added to the formation without the need to stop using those already in the formation, or without the need to recover the original satellite using the Space Shuttle.

Many of these satellites can be very small, weighing just a few tens of kilograms, and are therefore cheap to build and cheap to launch.

In **ASTRONOMY** multiple satellites at specific spacings make it possible to use them as a single giant telescope, just as multiple telescopes operate on the ground today (called giant arrays). The satellites that make up the NASA Starlight project apply this idea.

ASTRONOMY The study of space beyond the Earth and its contents.

GEOSTATIONARY SATELLITE A man-made satellite in a fixed or geosynchronous orbit around the Earth.

GEOSYNCHRONOUS ORBIT An orbit in which a satellite makes one circuit of the Earth in 24 hours.

GLOBAL POSITIONING SYSTEM A network of geostationary satellites that can be used to locate the position of any object on the Earth's surface.

GROUND STATION A receiving and transmitting station in direct communication with satellites. Such stations are characterized by having large dish-shaped antennae.

ROCKET ENGINE A propulsion system that burns liquid fuel such as liquid hydrogen.

SENSOR A device used to detect something.

SOLAR PANELS Large flat surfaces covered with thousands of small photoelectric devices that convert solar radiation into electricity.

TRANSPONDER Wireless receiver and transmitter.

Satellite sensors

Modern satellites can contain a wide variety of instruments. Some carry instruments we would recognize, such as a digital camera. It is useful on board a weather satellite (such as Tiros, Cosmos, and GOES) that needs to send back pictures of weather systems.

Communications satellites contain a **TRANSPONDER**—a receiver and transmitter that takes in information (such as your voice) at one **FREQUENCY** and then amplifies it and transmits it back to Earth on another frequency. Most satellites do not carry a single transponder but thousands. Just as with computer memory, the trick is to cram as much operating power into a small space as possible.

Other satellites carry detecting systems (**SENSORS**) according to what they are intended to do. For example, some may detect heat, others may send and receive **RADAR** waves, and so on. We will see examples of all of them later in this book.

FREQUENCY The number of complete cycles of (for example, radio) waves received per second.

RADAR Short for radio detecting and ranging. A system of bouncing radio waves from objects in order to map their surfaces and find out how far away they are.

SENSOR A device used to detect something.

TRANSPONDER Wireless receiver and transmitter.

◀▶ Satellite sensors can image either wide or narrow fields of view depending on the purpose of the view. Both pictures show the scene in Manhattan on 9/11. The picture on the left is a wide field of view of the New York area. This resolution helps display ground patterns. The picture on the right is a satellite view (not an aircraft view). But even this is not as close as satellites can get. Satellites can detect (see) objects smaller than a car.

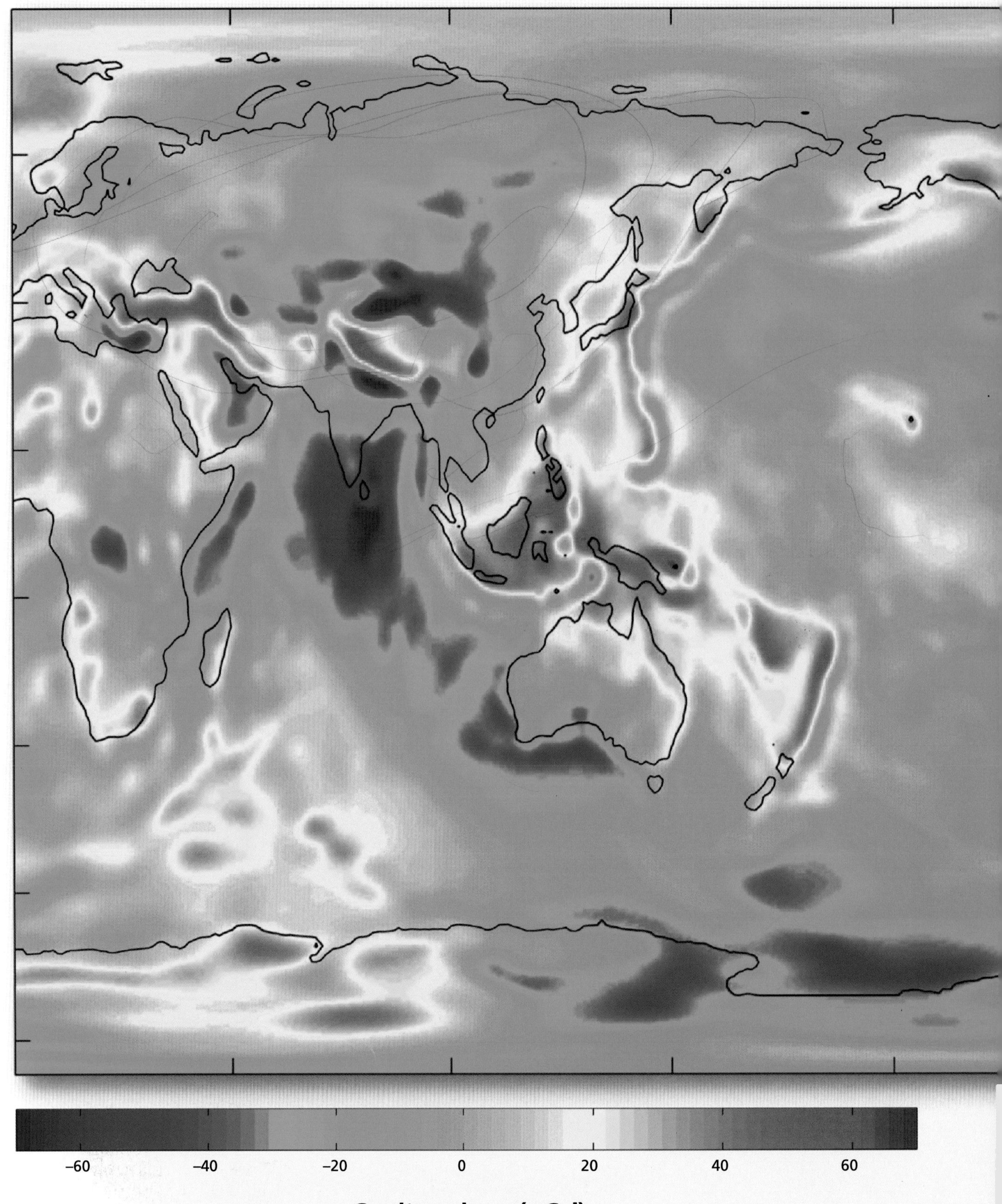
–60
–40
–20
0
20
40
60
Gravity variance (mGal)

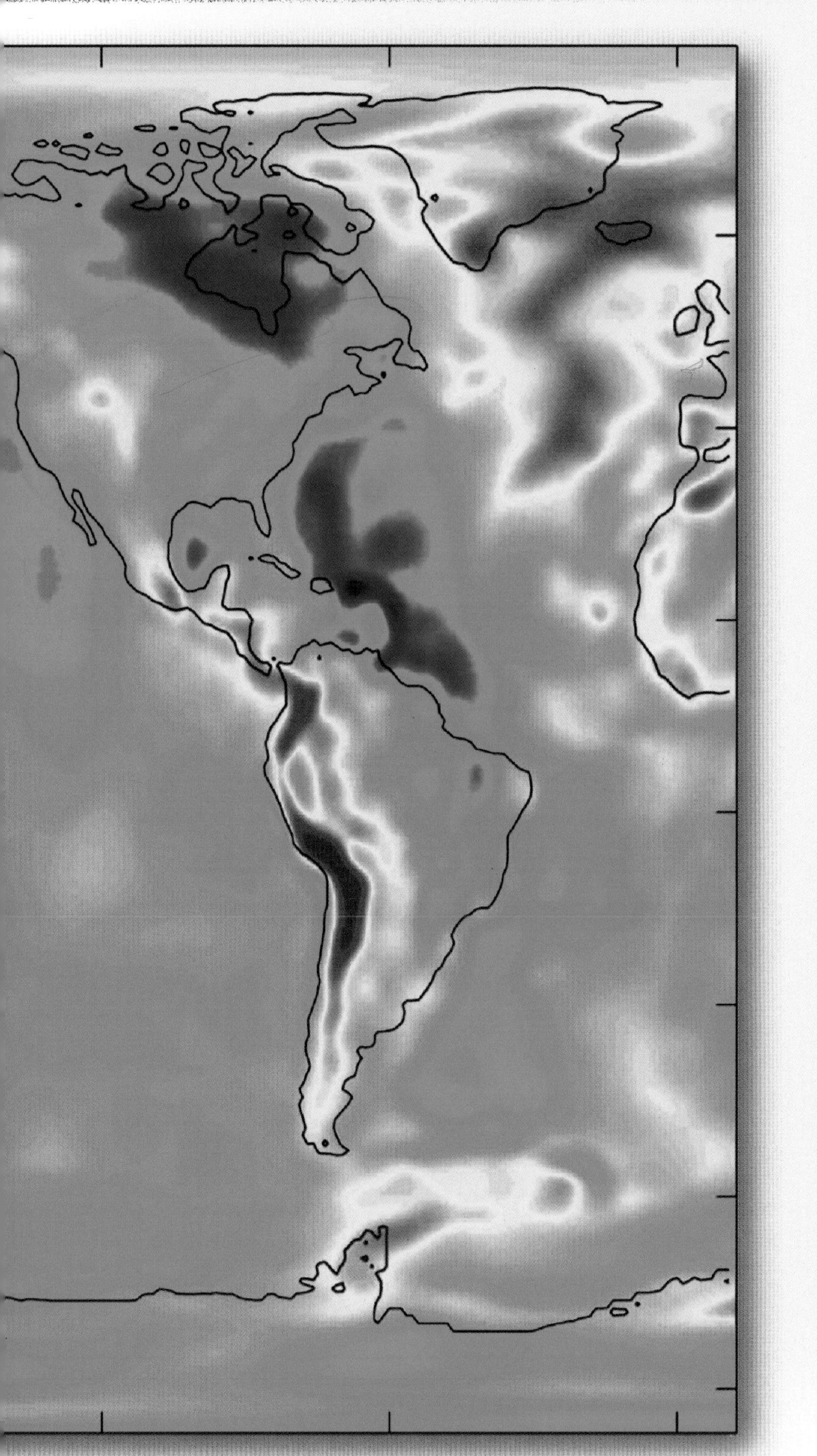

Power systems

To make the electronics work, a satellite must have a source of power. It is usually provided by panels of **SOLAR CELLS**, which top up rechargeable batteries.

Positioning and control

The basic detecting, transponding, or other system needs to be controlled. The positioning of the satellite also needs to be controlled. All of the satellites have an altitude control system to make sure the satellite keeps pointing the right way. All of these functions are carried out by a separate computer.

Positioning of satellites needs close control because over the equator, for example, there are hundreds of satellites in **GEOSYNCHRONOUS ORBIT**. It is like a space parking lot up there.

GEOSYNCHRONOUS ORBIT An orbit in which a satellite makes one circuit of the Earth in 24 hours.

GRAVITATIONAL PULL The force of attraction between bodies. The larger an object, the more its gravitational pull on other objects.

SOLAR CELL A photoelectric device that converts the energy from the Sun (solar radiation) into electrical energy.

▲ Sensors on satellites can detect the truly invisible. Grace is a satellite that senses minute variations in **GRAVITATIONAL PULL** from local changes in the Earth's mass by precisely measuring, to a tenth of the width of a human hair, changes in the separation of two identical spacecraft following the same orbit approximately 220 kilometers apart. Grace maps the variations from month to month, following changes produced by the seasons, weather patterns, and short-term climate change.

▲ The first Nimbus meteorological satellite was launched in 1964. The satellite was designed in two sections. The lower circular ring housed the weather sensors and electronics. The upper hexagonal section contained the altitude control system and had two **SOLAR PANELS** with 10,500 individual panels on each side. Nimbus-A weighed 380 kg and was made up of 40,000 components. A whole series of Nimbus satellites was launched in subsequent years.

2: LOOKING AT THE WEATHER AND OCEANS

The reason why meteorology (weather science) was an early user of satellite information was simple: To forecast the weather, you need to be able to see what is happening all across the world.

In the days before satellites meteorologists relied on a series of observing stations on land and a few on ships in the oceans. Because much of the moisture in the air is picked up from the oceans, having so little information about the weather over the oceans was a big handicap. For example, it was impossible to give a long period of notice of a hurricane as it moved toward the Caribbean or a typhoon as it moved toward Southeast Asia. Similarly, it was impossible to figure out what the weather would be like in areas affected by highs and lows (**ANTICYCLONES** and **DEPRESSIONS**) such as New York or Seattle or London, because most of the cloud associated with them formed over the sea.

Satellites add facts

Models of the way the atmosphere worked were also short of facts. For example, people thought that weather patterns in one region of the world were unrelated to those elsewhere.

However, as soon as the first satellites brought back pictures of cloud patterns from space, it was very clear that the entire world's weather patterns were linked. Since then worldwide ocean and weather changes such as **EL NIÑO** and **LA NIÑA** have become well known.

◀ Tiros, first launched in 1960, provided the first accurate weather forecasts based on data gathered from space. Tiros was NASA's first step to see if satellites could be useful to study the Earth.

▼ A deep depression, or low-pressure region, sucks in air from the ocean and swirls it around, dragging it ever higher as though it were riding a corkscrew. As the air rises, it cools. Its moisture turns to water droplets, and clouds form. In this way the pattern of clouds shows what the atmosphere is doing, as in this depression moving into the United Kingdom and Ireland along the western coast of Europe.

▲ This satellite image shows a very intense depression over Hudson Bay in Canada. A huge cold front is wrapped around the core of the depression. Below the bands of cloud extensive rain is falling. To the left and below, the cloud is more broken. This is what cumulus cloud looks like from a satellite.

ANTICYCLONE A roughly circular region of the atmosphere that is spiraling outward and downward.

DEPRESSION A region of inward swirling air in the atmosphere associated with cloudy weather and rain.

EL NIÑO A time when ocean currents in the Pacific Ocean reverse from their normal pattern and disrupt global weather patterns. It occurs once every 4 or 5 years.

LA NIÑA Below normal ocean temperatures in the eastern Pacific Ocean that disrupt global weather patterns.

SOLAR PANELS Large flat surfaces covered with thousands of small photoelectric devices that convert solar radiation into electricity.

Messages in the clouds

The nature of clouds was well understood before satellites were invented. But what satellites could do was to provide a pattern of the clouds and also to identify their height, thickness, and how much rain they were producing. As a result, meteorologists became much more accurate with their short-term weather forecasts.

But simply looking at clouds using ordinary visible light gives us just part of the picture. From satellites it is also possible to see the air in other ways. For example, **INFRARED** pictures are routinely taken in order to see through the clouds to areas of rain, while images of **WATER VAPOR** give a view not only of where it is moist and dry but also of the way the air is moving.

▲ Satellite images can show things about the atmosphere that we simply cannot see. This is a global view of the water vapor in the air, using red as the color for the image. Notice the swirling patterns near the top and bottom of the image. They are depressions.

◀ Hurricanes, also known as typhoons and tropical cyclones, are the world's most powerful weather systems. They are spawned in the tropics, close to the equator, and then spin off north or south over the oceans. As they do this, they pick up huge amounts of moisture and suck it higher and higher until it turns into water droplets. As this happens, the water gives out heat, which fuels the hurricane and makes it even more powerful. In the center of a hurricane is a region of calm, clear air called the eye. You can see a hurricane in this picture (Hurricane Lili) in the Caribbean. Florida is near the top of the picture; South America is at the bottom left.

Weather satellites

Weather satellite systems fall into two types: **GEOSTATIONARY SATELLITES** called geostationary operational environmental satellites (GOES) for short-range warning and "now-casting," and polar-orbiting satellites for longer-term forecasting.

GOES satellites, the first of which was launched in 1975, provide the kind of continuous monitoring necessary for intensive data analysis. They circle the Earth in a **GEOSYNCHRONOUS ORBIT**, hovering continuously over one position on the surface, 35,786 km above the Earth. By coincidence this also provides close to a full disk view of the Earth. By continuously covering the whole Earth, operators can spot sudden changes in the weather, especially those likely to cause severe events such as hurricanes and floods. GOES satellites are able to monitor storm development and track its movements.

GEOSTATIONARY SATELLITE A man-made satellite in a fixed or geosynchronous orbit around the Earth.

GEOSYNCHRONOUS ORBIT An orbit in which a satellite makes one circuit of the Earth in 24 hours.

INFRARED Radiation with a wavelength that is longer than red light.

RADAR Short for radio detecting and ranging. A system of bouncing radio waves from objects in order to map their surfaces and find out how far away they are.

WATER VAPOR The gaseous form of water. Also sometimes referred to as moisture.

◀ This is a cyclone moving up the Bay of Bengal. A picture taken in visible light shows the cyclone clearly, but it is not possible to know what is going on inside the cyclone from this image.

However, by using **RADAR**, it is possible to see through the cloud to measure the amount of rain that is falling and to see the structure of the cyclone. From this it is much easier to predict what the cyclone might do and therefore the chances of damage when it reaches land. The colored strip across this picture shows a part of a scan made by a satellite using precipitation radar. The increased detail is startling.

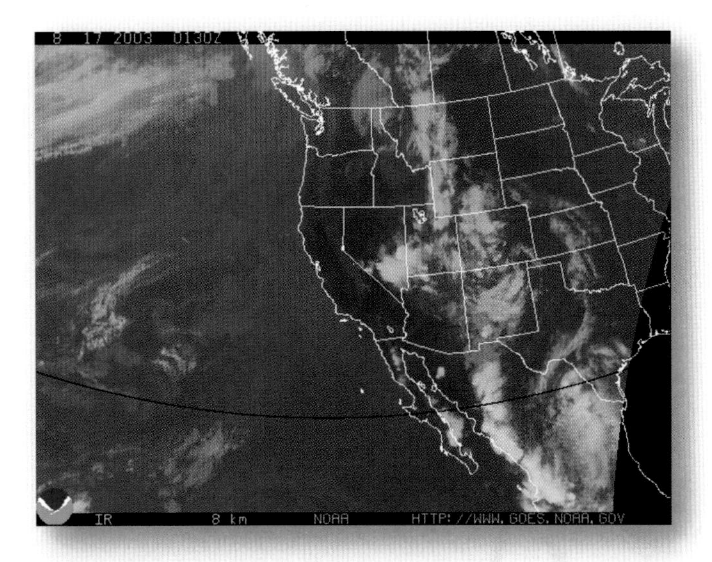

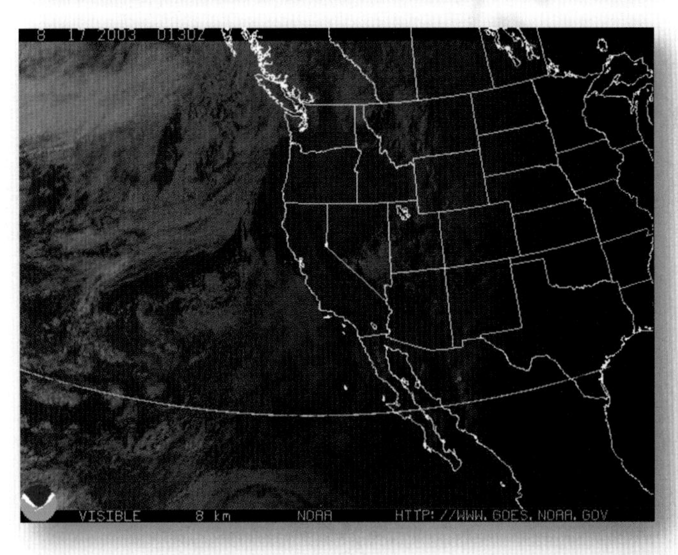

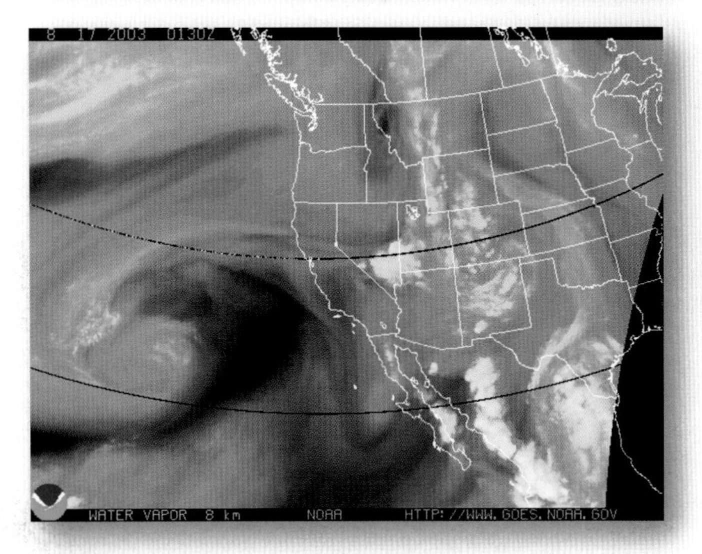

▲ Color-enhanced GOES view shows the nearly pole-to-pole coverage.

◀ The same satellite view of the eastern Pacific Ocean seen in visible light (*top*), infrared (*middle*), and using a sensor designed to detect water vapor (*bottom*). Images like these show meteorologists what is happening in the atmosphere and help them predict the weather.

▼ Color-enhanced imagery is a method meteorologists use to aid them with satellite interpretation. The colors enable a meteorologist to easily and quickly see features that are of special interest to them. Usually they look for high clouds or areas with a large amount of water vapor.

In an infrared image cold clouds are high clouds, so the colors typically highlight the colder regions. In a water vapor image white areas indicate moisture, and dark areas point to little or no moisture, so typically the colors highlight areas with large amounts of moisture.

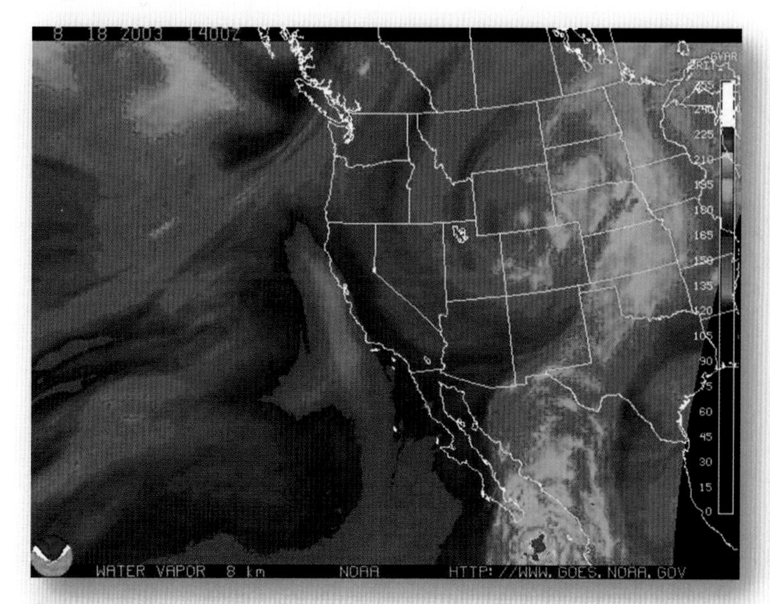

Color-enhanced image of the eastern Pacific, showing areas of low moisture, water vapor (orange), and high water vapor (green).

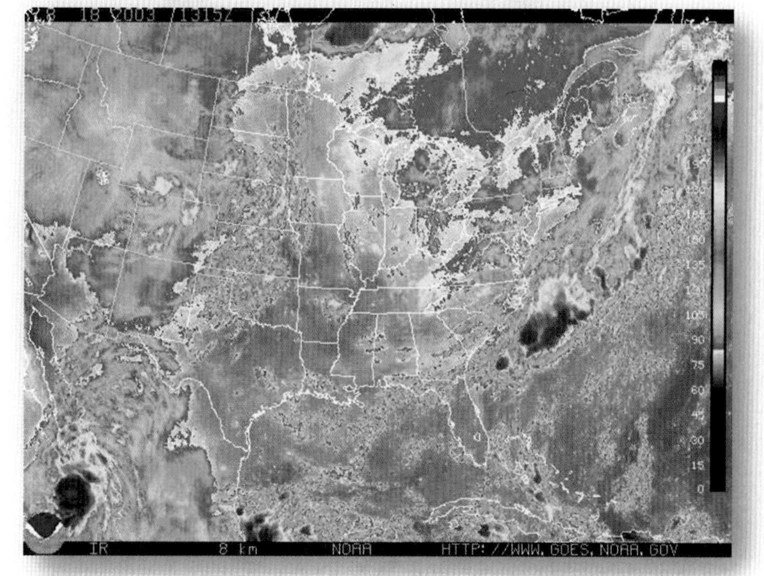

An infrared image of North America designed to show places where there is a high intensity of precipitation (yellows to reds). In this image there is a depression between North America and Russia and another one off the East Coast of the United States and Canada.

The GOES satellites are operated by the United States. Other countries have similar satellites for observing other parts of the world. For example, the European Union operates Meteosat. Information is shared among satellite providers.

GOES satellite imagery is also used to estimate rainfall during thunderstorms and hurricanes to provide flash-flood warnings, as well as to estimate snowfall accumulations and overall extent of snow cover. Satellite sensors also map the movements of sea and lake ice.

▲ One of the main tasks of a geostationary weather satellite is to track weather systems. This is a view created by superimposing three images of Hurricane Andrew (1992) to show its change in position and size as it tracked over Florida.

Instruments on GOES

There are two main GOES instruments—the imager and the sounder. The imager senses direct **RADIATION** from the Earth and reflected **SOLAR** energy from the Earth's surface and atmosphere. The sounder provides data to determine the vertical temperature and moisture profile of the atmosphere, surface and cloud top temperatures, and **OZONE** distribution.

Polar-orbiting satellites

Complementing the **GEOSTATIONARY SATELLITES** are polar-orbiting satellites. The United States' satellites are called Tiros (advanced television infrared observation satellite). Such satellites constantly circle the Earth in an almost north-south orbit, passing close to both poles. The orbits are circular, with an altitude of between 830 (morning orbit) and 870 (afternoon orbit) km, and are Sun **SYNCHRONOUS**. One satellite crosses the equator at 7:30 A.M. local time, the other at 1:40 P.M. local time. Operating as a pair, these satellites ensure that data for any region of the Earth is no more than 6 hours old.

The satellites provide visible and **INFRARED** data that can be used for making images of the atmosphere and for finding out temperature conditions in the air. **ULTRAVIOLET** sensors have been able to detect the lack of ozone gas near the poles (known as the **OZONE HOLE**).

GEOSTATIONARY SATELLITE A man-made satellite in a fixed or geosynchronous orbit around the Earth.

INFRARED Radiation with a wavelength that is longer than red light.

OZONE A form of oxygen (O_3) with three atoms in each molecule instead of the more usual two (O_2).

OZONE HOLE The observed lack of the gas ozone in the upper atmosphere.

RADIATION The transfer of energy in the form of waves (such as light and heat) or particles (such as from radioactive decay of a material).

SOLAR Anything to do with the Sun.

SYNCHRONOUS Taking place at the same time.

ULTRAVIOLET A form of radiation that is just beyond the violet end of the visible spectrum and so is called "ultra" (more than) violet. At the other end of the visible spectrum is "infra" (less than) red.

▼▶ These two maps show how a satellite can capture air or sea surface temperature quickly over large areas. The bottom picture shows regions of Europe that experienced much hotter than normal land temperatures in 2003, while the picture on the right shows regions of the Atlantic seaboard of the United States, which were much colder than average. These pictures were taken by the moderate-resolution imaging spectroradiometer (MODIS) instrument on the Terra satellite.

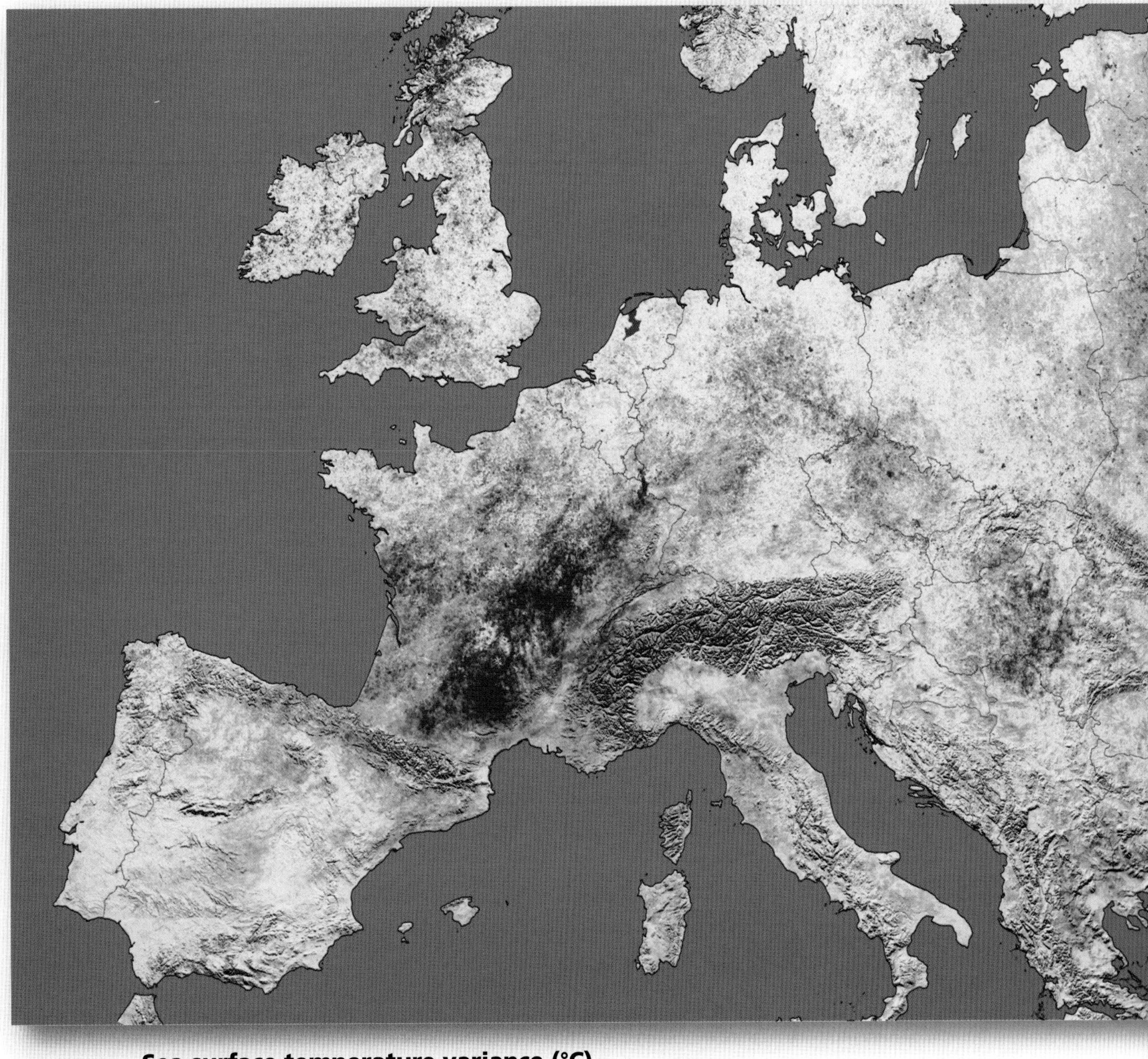

Sea surface temperature variance (°C)

–5 0 +5

3: WHAT THE EARTH LOOKS LIKE

People have always been curious about what the Earth looks like. But how were they to find out?

The invention of the camera meant that, at last, people could keep visual records of everything around them. If they took a camera with them in a hot air balloon, they would be able to look down on and record the Earth's surface for the first time in history.

Cameras

A camera works by capturing the light reflected, or bounced back, from an object or transmitted by it, focusing it through a lens and using the light to produce a change in the pattern of chemicals on a film or a glass plate.

In the earliest photographs the sensitive surface was made using silver salts, and the result was a black-and-white negative, which then had to be turned into a positive by printing it onto specially prepared paper.

By the 1840s pictures taken from balloons were being called aerial photographs. A start had been made.

▶ In 1974 the first-ever photo map of the contiguous 48 states of the United States was prepared from satellite images taken in 1972. It used 595 cloud-free black-and-white images returned from NASA's first Earth resources technology satellite (ERTS-1). The images were all taken at the same altitude (912 km) and at the same lighting angle.

Aircraft

With the invention of the airplane in the early 1900s the scene was set for another step forward. By World War I reconnaissance planes were flying over enemy lines and photographing the location of troops. These were the first military spy missions, and they immediately focused people's minds on how useful—and finally how profitable—it could be to look down on the Earth.

▶ The very first view of Earth taken by the Explorer satellite was not much to look at, but it was an important first step. In this picture you can see the lines scanned by the camera.

Rockets

From World War I until the 1960s the aerial photograph remained the only way to look down onto the Earth. But looking down was not confined to aircraft. After World War II some V2 **ROCKETS** were used to get high-altitude pictures of the Earth. The U.S. Army called this the Viking program (a term that would be used for spaceflight in later decades).

These were the first views to show the curvature of the Earth, but their scope was very limited.

ROCKET Any kind of device that uses the principle of jet propulsion, that is, the rapid release of gases designed to propel an object rapidly.

More on the V2 and other rockets can be found in Volume 6: *Journey into space*.

Nevertheless, already the term for taking pictures from the air was changing as scientists realized that many properties of the Earth's surface could be discovered by photography without actually visiting the sites. Thus the term remote sensing came about.

Satellites

In 1957 the world changed forever with the launching of Sputnik 1. Although Sputnik 1 was not able to look down on the Earth, its successful launching proved the possibility of getting an object into space. And if the object carried a camera, and the camera could be recovered or linked to a transmitter, it would soon be possible to see the Earth from space.

During the 1960s manned spaceflight became a reality, and astronauts and **COSMONAUTS** were able to take pictures from space. Yet these random pictures were not the most valuable way of looking down on the Earth. For this, untiring **SATELLITES** have the edge.

As a result, in the 1960s special satellites were designed, built, and put into **ORBIT**. At first they were just basically high-altitude cameras; they were black and white, and their image resolution (the amount of detail they could capture) was poor.

▼ This electronic still-camera photo of the Chilean/Argentinian Andes Mountains was taken from the **INTERNATIONAL SPACE STATION** in late spring, when most of the previous winter's snow had melted below an altitude of 2,000 m.

You can clearly see a wide variety of landforms such as glaciated valleys and pyramidal mountain peaks. The sharp, glaciated crest of the Cerro San Lorenzo (*center*) exceeds 4,000 m and casts a long shadow southeastward.

Glacial data collected over the past 50 years suggests that small ice bodies are disappearing at accelerating rates. Predictions are that large melting of land ice, with perhaps major flooding resulting, is possible in the coming decades and centuries. Before glacial data can be used to address critical problems, more detailed information about such glaciers is needed. Images like this from the International Space Station can be added to those taken from vertically sensing satellites to provide information on glaciers in remote areas around the world.

▲ The simplest way of observing the land from space is to use a hand-held camera. This picture, showing the eruption of Mt. Etna in southern Italy, was taken by an astronaut in the International Space Station. It is known as an oblique view.

For more on the history of satellites see Volume 6: *Journey into space*.

COSMONAUT A Russian space person.

INTERNATIONAL SPACE STATION The international orbiting space laboratory.

ORBIT The path followed by one object as it tracks around another.

SATELLITE A man-made object that orbits the Earth.

▲ This is a picture of the Himalaya Mountains in Asia. The central peak is Mt. Everest. From the satellite's vantage point it is possible to see the extent of the glaciers stretching away from the mountains and, from year to year, to see how they change in size.

▲ This is a true-color picture of the Nile River and its delta. It was taken by a moderate-resolution imaging spectroradiometer (MODIS) instrument.

Multispectral images

When you look at an ordinary picture in visible light, you get the whole spectrum combined (as white light). But it is possible to subdivide the range, just as when you use color filters on a camera. If you use a red filter and black-and-white film, wherever red light enters the filter, it is allowed through. When the film is printed, all objects that were red show up as white. At the same time, the red filter blocks green and blue light. If we put a green filter on the lens, we can see patterns that were green; and by using a blue filter, we can see patterns that were blue.

Now we have three black-and-white images that represent red, green, and blue light reaching the film.

Although it might at first seem strange to filter out the light in this way, it is, in fact, how most modern color digital cameras and satellite sensors work. Each sensor is sensitive to just one primary color. That allows it to collect simpler data, which is easier than trying to take the whole spectrum. It therefore needs less memory, the data can be sent faster from satellites, and so on. All that needs to be done is to build up the picture in reverse, and a color image results.

▼ New Zealand shown in true color using the moderate-resolution imaging spectroradiometer (MODIS). You can see the mountains and coastal plain under the cloud. The bright blue around part of the coast may be a bloom of microscopic plants called algae.

False-color composites

Instead of trying to reproduce the exact visual image, we can use an INFRARED image to replace one of the original colors. Infrared highlights, for example, any healthy vegetation as bright tones. By using this different, nonvisual image, we now make a picture not with ordinary colors, but instead create new colors that serve different purposes. These images are called FALSE-COLOR composites. Various kinds of vegetation now show up in several tones of red, pink, or yellow (where red is healthy vegetation, and pink and yellow are failing growth).

Here are two examples of how this is used. In a military context suppose the enemy has put tanks on the ground and has used camouflage nets to hide them from the air. They may not appear in visible-light pictures; but by using false color, the camouflage nets will show up as a different (dark) color than the vegetation around it.

A second example involves scientists trying to find out where a forest is growing healthily. The healthy trees show red, others pink and yellow. In this way it is easy to see if there is any pattern to the unhealthy growth.

Landsat

Landsat is a powerful way of looking at the Earth's surface that has many applications for geologists, hydrologists (scientists who study water), and biologists. By 1972 NASA had developed a satellite with sensors to produce false-color images. It was called ERTS-1 (Earth resources technology satellite) and was launched on July 23, 1972. It has subsequently been renamed Landsat.

Seven Landsat satellites have been launched. The orbits of all Landsats are near-polar and Sun-SYNCHRONOUS (they go over the equator every orbit between 9:30 and 10:00 A.M.), making 14 passes southward from the North Pole each day (taking about 103 minutes for a complete orbit). After any given orbit the spacecraft will be 2,875 km to the west of where it was at the start of the orbit. It takes about 11,000 shots to image the entire Earth's land surface.

▶ Terkezi Oasis, Chad, image was acquired by Landsat 7's enhanced thematic mapper plus (ETM+). This is a false-color composite image made using near infrared, green, and red wavelengths.

FALSE COLOR The colors used to make the appearance of some property more obvious.

INFRARED Radiation with a wavelength that is longer than red light.

SYNCHRONOUS Taking place at the same time.

Applications

Landsat has been one of the most valuable Earth-surveying satellites. For instance, investigators used Landsat images of California's Imperial Valley to count more than 25 separate crops in 8,865 fields covering 458,000 acres in only 45 hours of flight. This experiment and others demonstrated the potential of satellite systems for swift and frequent inventories, which are fundamental to accurate crop forecasting. Good forecasts are a big help in planning the amounts of labor, fuel, and transportation needed for harvest and distribution.

Landsat imagery of water circulation and sand and mud patterns along seacoasts have also been used to devise a strategy for deploying equipment to contain oil spills.

▼ A Landsat image of parts of Maryland, Pennsylvania, New Jersey, and Delaware. The main rivers are the Susquehanna (*top left*) and the Delaware (*top right*), and the largest cities are Philadelphia (*top right*) and Baltimore (*left of center*). In the top left-hand corner you can see the ridges of the Appalachian Mountains. Chesapeake Bay is to the left. Notice how the silt in Delaware Bay (*right*) shows pink. Sand dunes show as purple. The cities show gray.

Information about **FAULTS** and **FRACTURE** zones derived from Landsat imagery has been used in the United States and abroad to select locations for new power plants and to determine the best routes for oil and gas pipelines. The satellite imagery has also been used by Alaska to aid navigation in Cook Inlet, by California to select recreational areas, and by Japan to monitor pollution in Osaka Bay.

FAULT A place in the crust where rocks have fractured, and then one side has moved relative to the other.

FRACTURE A break in brittle rock.

▲ The Lena River Delta is on the Arctic Ocean coast of Russia. The Lena River (4,400 km long) is the most extensive, protected wilderness area in Russia. This image was acquired by Landsat 7's enhanced thematic mapper plus (ETM+) sensor. This is a false-color composite image made using shortwave infrared, infrared, and red wavelengths.

The river flows in from the bottom of the picture, with the ocean at the top. Notice how all of the delta waterways (known as distributaries) show clearly as deep blue, with sandbanks showing as purple. Numerous small lakes also show on the left. Each different type of plant is shown by a contrasting color.

In the late 1970s a prolonged drought brought starvation and death to millions of people in the Sahel, a vast African prairie just south of the Sahara Desert. The desert has been creeping steadily south for years, eliminating the marginal livelihood offered by the dry prairie. At the request of a number of countries in the area Landsat surveyed the Sahel; its photographs dramatically illustrated the problem. A polygonal-shaped patch of vegetation stood out from the surrounding dry, parched land: It was an enclosed, fenced ranch, where careful management had prevented the livestock from overgrazing and wearing away the land. Landsat pictures have helped Alaska Indians select thousands of acres of timberland and mineral exploration areas from vast wilderness tracts offered by the federal government to settle native claims going back to 1867, when the United States purchased Alaska from Russia.

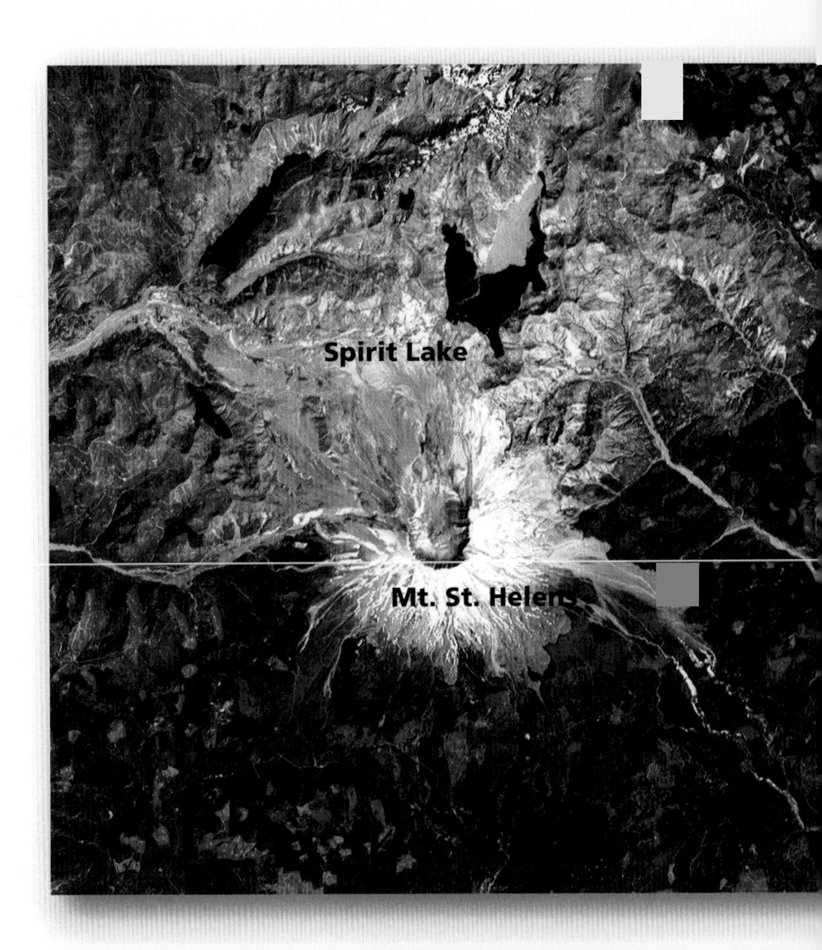

▲ Compare these pictures of damage from the Mt. St. Helens volcanic eruption. The one at the top of page 39 is taken from a Space Shuttle with an ordinary camera in visible light. The one directly above is a false-color Landsat picture. The false-color picture makes the area of destruction much clearer. Dark green is undamaged and uncut forest.

Geographers also used Landsat. In remote Antarctica Landsat cameras revealed previously unknown groups of mountains in southern Victoria Land and at the head of the Lambert Glacier. They also disclosed significant changes in the location of Burke Island, in the size and position of the Thwaites Iceberg Tongue, and in long stretches of the Antarctic coastline.

Landsat can also identify and monitor the accumulation of winter snows in the mountains and can help estimate the springtime runoff from melting snow.

Landsat imagery has been used to help government and private organizations assess flood damage and plan disaster relief and flood-control programs.

Landsat images clearly show ice types and the distribution, growth, movement, and breakup of sea ice. Shippers can then learn which ports are ice free and can chart courses through open waters in largely ice-covered seas.

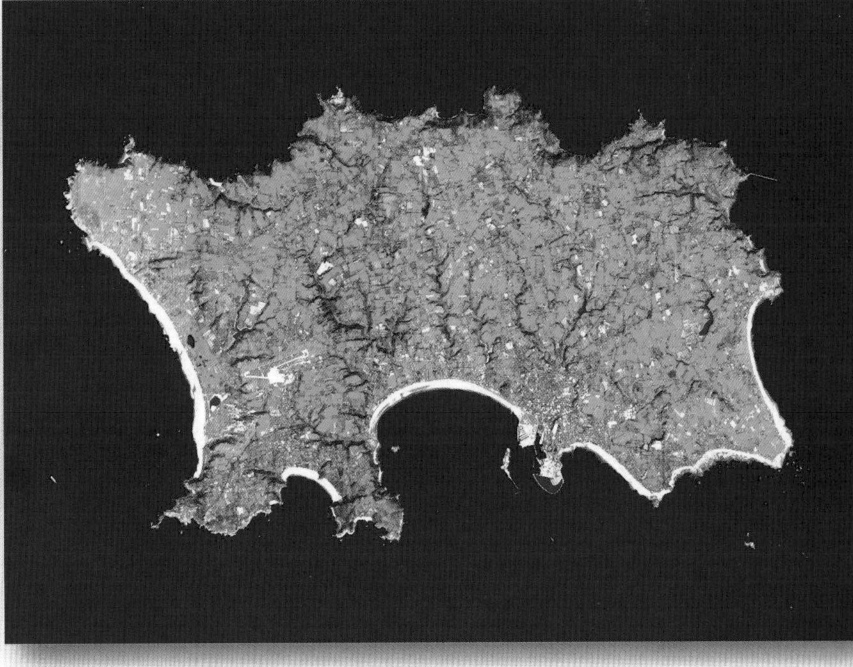

▶ Landsat views allow a perspective on the pattern of land use of the fields on the island of Jersey, off the French coast.

◀ This scene covers an area that is 54 x 57 km. It was acquired by the advanced space-borne thermal emission and reflection radiometer (ASTER) aboard NASA's Terra satellite.

It shows, in false color, the Mississippi River entering the Gulf of Mexico, where it loses energy and dumps its load of sediment to form its delta.

The area shown in this false-color image is the currently active delta front of the Mississippi. The migratory nature of the delta forms natural traps for oil. Most of the land in the image consists of mudflats and marshlands. There is little human settlement in this area due to the instability of the sediments. The main shipping channel of the Mississippi River is the broad stripe running from northwest to southeast.

Thermal imaging

The land gives out heat, which is, in part, a property of the material from which the surface is made. The atmosphere absorbs much of the heat, except in certain narrow wavelength "windows." By using these windows, land, water, ice, and the atmosphere can all be investigated. NASA's instrument called TIMS (thermal infrared multispectral scanner) produces images that are very colorful as well as useful. However, to know exactly what the colors mean, scientists still have to visit some sample ground sites and then match colors to ground observations. You can imagine that a few spot-checks save a lot of time, effort, and money compared with having to survey the whole region on foot. Petroleum geologists are among many who value this information when prospecting in remote areas.

◀ The moderate-resolution imaging spectroradiometer (MODIS) on the Aqua satellite picks out features like the dozens of large fires burning across the Rocky Mountains in Canada (*top*), Montana (*bottom right*), and Idaho (*bottom center*). The sources of the fires have been subsequently marked with red dots.

▲ This MODIS picture shows strong winds blowing Sahara Desert dust from Libya and Egypt out across the Mediterranean Sea.

▼ This is a natural-colored mosaic of Scandinavia and the Baltic region taken using the multiangle imaging spectroradiometer's (MISR) vertical-viewing camera. The camera took pictures of the surface but did not make **TOPOGRAPHY** measurements. To get this 3D image, the information was draped over a shaded relief digital terrain elevation model from the United States Geological Survey.

The MISR observes the daylit Earth continuously from pole to pole and every 9 days views the entire globe between 82°N and 82°S latitude.

TOPOGRAPHY The shape of the land surface in terms of height.

▼ This image was made by the advanced spaceborne thermal emission and reflection radiometer (ASTER) on NASA's Terra satellite. It shows the geology of the Atlas Mountains of North Africa in false color.

These mountains are made of many bands of different kinds of rock that have been folded and then eroded during the long history of the range.

In this ASTER image short-wavelength infrared (SWIR) bands are combined to dramatically highlight the different rock types and to illustrate the complex folding. The yellowish, orange, and green areas are limestones, sandstones, and gypsum; the dark-blue and green areas are underlying granitic rocks. The ability to map geology using ASTER data is enhanced by the multiple SWIR bands, which are sensitive to differences in rock composition.

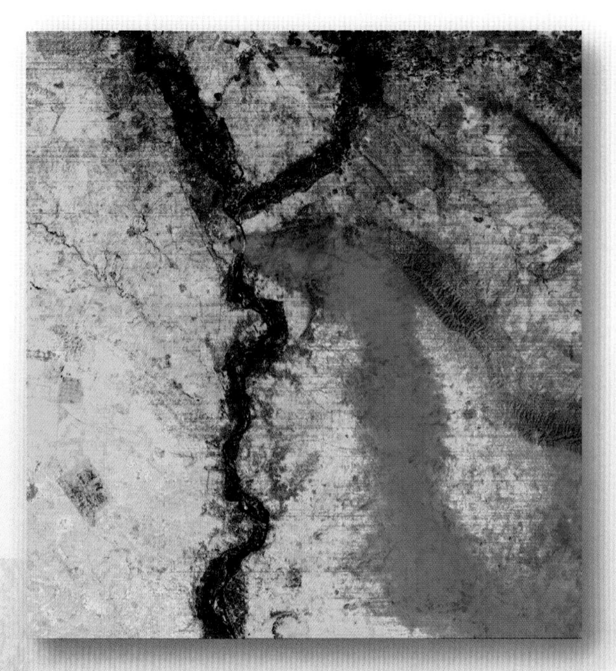

▲ ASTER detecting a sulfur dioxide plume (purple) rising above a fire in Baghdad, Iraq. The dark line is the Tigris River.

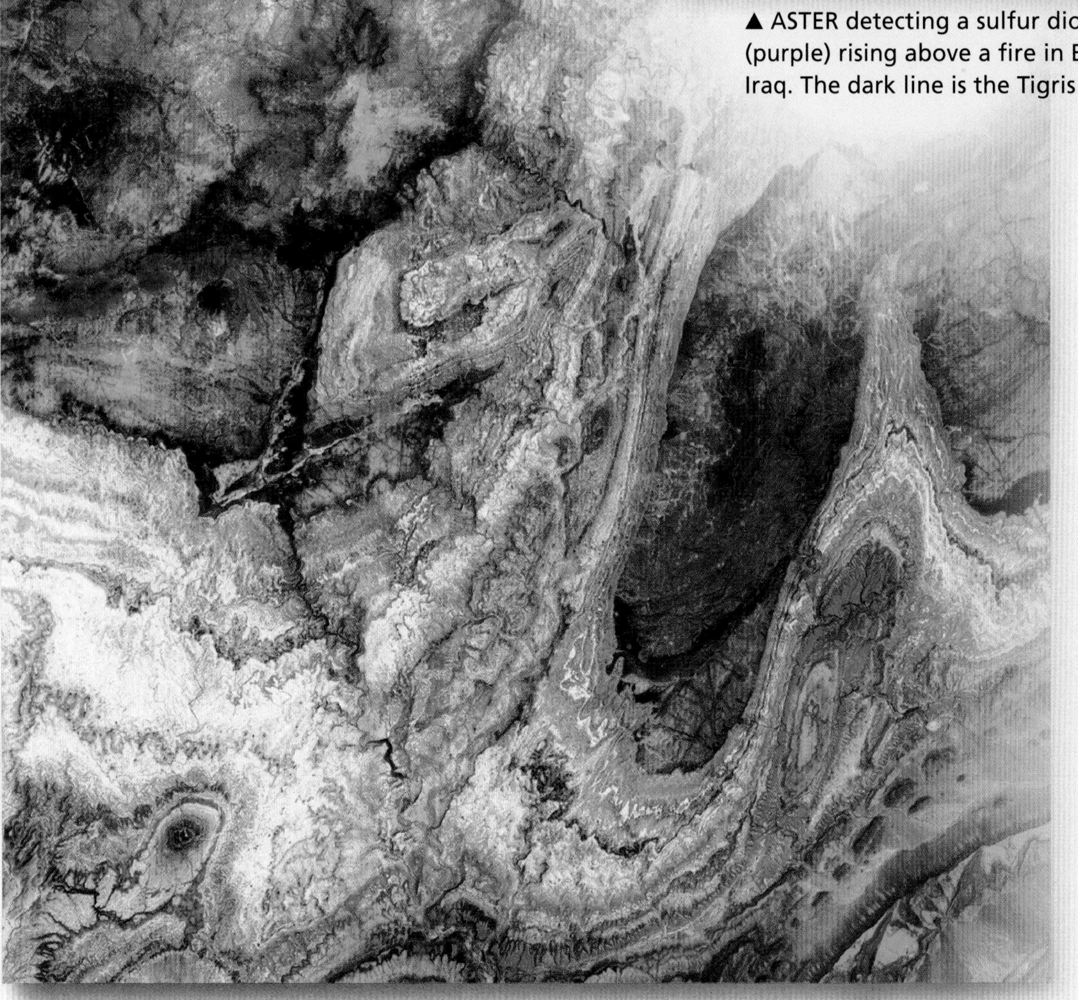

Radar

RADAR is another method for investigating the Earth's surface. Its big advantage is that it can penetrate clouds. **SPACE SHUTTLE** missions have included radar projects.

Radar commonly provides a very different view of the same landscape compared with a visible image. Pictures by ASTER, for example, can be compared with those produced by Landsat and ground-based data.

▶ Satellite images can be used on their own or combined with data from other sources to create perspectives that would otherwise not be possible. This is a composite image of the Grand Canyon in Colorado created by using height information made into a 3D model and then superimposing it with Landsat data. The view looks west. Green indicates forest; pinks and purples indicate bare rock. The data does not allow a geological interpretation. A photo from the Grand Canyon is shown above for comparison.

Two satellites can "see" quite different things in the same scene. Compare the two pictures, the one on the left taken by ASTER, the one above using Landsat information.

RADAR Short for radio detecting and ranging. A system of bouncing radio waves from objects in order to map their surfaces and find out how far away they are.

SPACE SHUTTLE NASA's reusable space vehicle that is launched like a rocket but returns like a glider.

▶ Cotopaxi Volcano, Ecuador, was taken by the shuttle radar topography mission (SRTM). It is more than 3,000 m higher than its surroundings. The base has a width of about 23 km.

The digital elevation model acquired by SRTM, with its resolution of 25 m x 25 m, is so rich in detail that you can even make out an inner crater with a diameter of 120 m x 250 m inside the outer crater (800 m x 650 m). Blue and green correspond to the lowest elevations in the image, while beige, orange, red, and white represent increasing elevations. Monitoring volcanoes from space on a regular basis can be helpful in predicting hazards to nearby populations.

▼ This is a picture of the earthquake-prone Los Angeles region of California.

This image shows the earthquake faults that lie between the mountains and the lowlands. The San Andreas Fault, the largest fault in California, divides the very rugged San Gabriel Mountains from the low-relief Mojave Desert.

To make this image, hill shading from the SRTM (shuttle radar topography mission, which is housed on a Space Shuttle) was added to a Landsat image, and a false Sun illumination was added from the left (southwest). Fault data are from the United States Geological Survey.

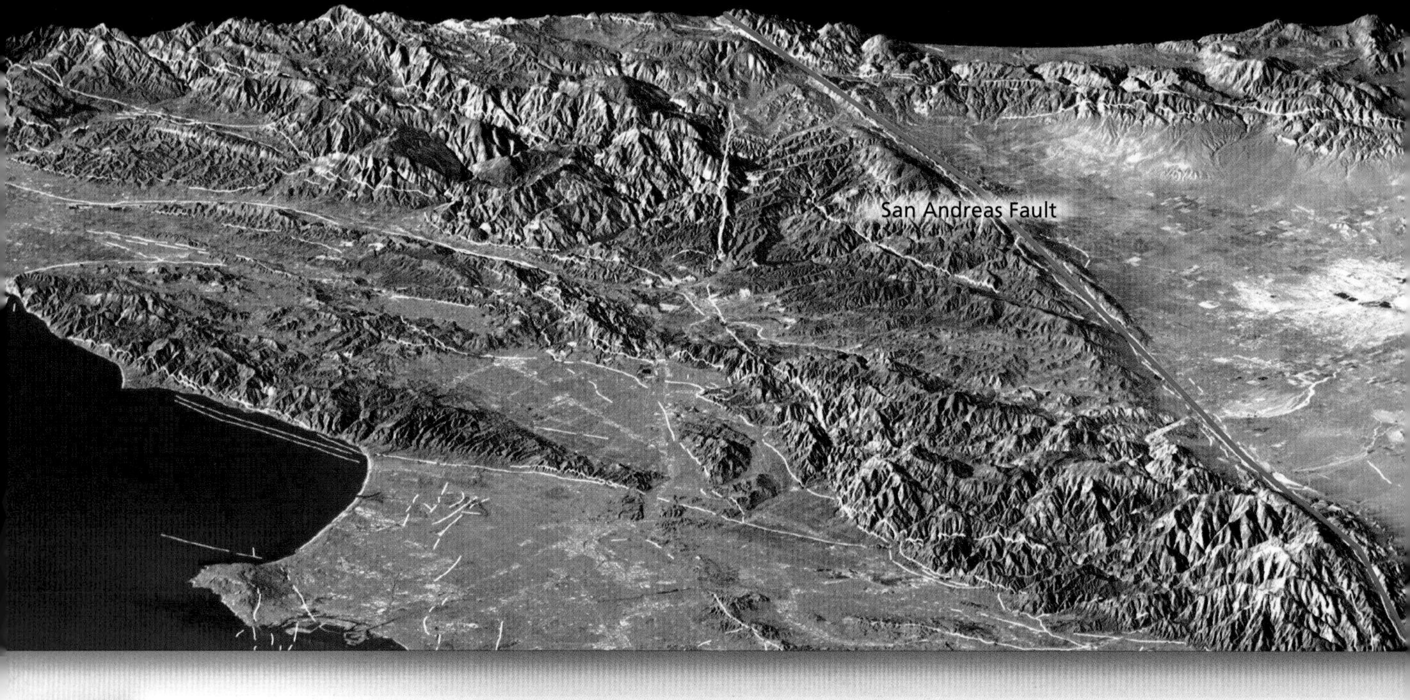

Of special note is the shuttle radar topography mission (SRTM), which is a project run on the Space Shuttle with the objective of mapping the Earth in 3D (three dimensions).

If you are going to map anything in 3D, you have to know two things: the distance to the object and its position. From a satellite the distance is a measure of the height.

The most common way of finding distances and heights in land-based surveying is by the method of triangles. It is a property of the geometry of a triangle that if you know the length of all three of its sides, there is only one shape of triangle you can draw. The same is true if you know one length and two angles of the triangle. The construction of triangles is thus a simple, but powerful and foolproof, way of surveying.

Traditionally, a baseline was set out, and then the angles to points of interest were measured, one set at one end of the baseline, the other set at the other end of the baseline. Since the baseline (one side of a triangle) and two angles to a third point were now known, the point can be located accurately.

However, you do not have to use an **OPTICAL** instrument for this—you can use **RADIO WAVES**. Just like light waves, radio waves bounce off objects, and the reflected wave can be detected. This is the principle of radar, which has been used for more than half a century.

In this case a transmitter sends the signal, and a receiver in the same place receives some of the reflected wave. At the simplest level you might send just a "ping." A fraction of a second later your receiver might hear the reflection of the ping. By knowing the time between transmission and reception, you can figure out the distance.

Now combine these ideas of surveying and using radar, and you can see that it is possible to use radar for surveying.

But how do you use the radar to find all the points of detail that you want for your map? The answer is to make a broad transmission and a broad collection (that is, make a picture), and then use powerful computers to sort out the result.

▲▶ Here you can see the principle of triangulation for a valley bottom and for a mountain top. The triangles are different shapes.

ANTENNA (pl. **ANTENNAE**) A device used for sending out and receiving radio waves.

OPTICAL Relating to the use of light.

RADIO WAVES A form of electromagnetic radiation, like light and heat. Radio waves have a longer wavelength than light waves.

The SRTM does it this way. The main transmitting **ANTENNA** is located in the payload bay of the Space Shuttle. The transmitter illuminates a portion of the surface of the Earth with a beam of radar waves just as a searchlight illuminates the ground with visible light waves. The transmitting antenna also acts as a receiving antenna, while another is placed way out on a 60-meter mast.

▲ This image of France was produced using information from the shuttle radar topography mission (SRTM)—see page 52. The data acquired was then manipulated to fit on a map projection type called mercator.

Both shading and color coding of topographic height have been used. The shade image was derived by computing relief slope in the northwest-southeast direction, so that northwest slopes appear bright, and southeast slopes appear dark. Color coding is directly related to topographic height, with green at the lower elevations, rising through yellow and tan, to white at the highest elevations.

Now you have a known baseline (one side of a triangle that is 60 m long) and two receiving antennae, one at each end. The setup for triangulation is in place.

RADAR Short for radio detecting and ranging. A system of bouncing radio waves from objects in order to map their surfaces and find out how far away they are.

Interferometry

Sorting out the data as it comes back uses another idea, called interferometry. In interferometry two images of the same area (**RADAR** pictures) are taken from different vantage points. There will be slight differences in the two images.

The colored pattern you get is similar to that of a puddle of water with a film of oil on it. When two interferometric radar data sets are combined, the first product made is called an interferogram with these colored bands on it (also called a fringe map). A computer can make use of this interferogram to produce a 3D map.

▼ An interferogram from which a 3D image can be compiled using powerful computers.

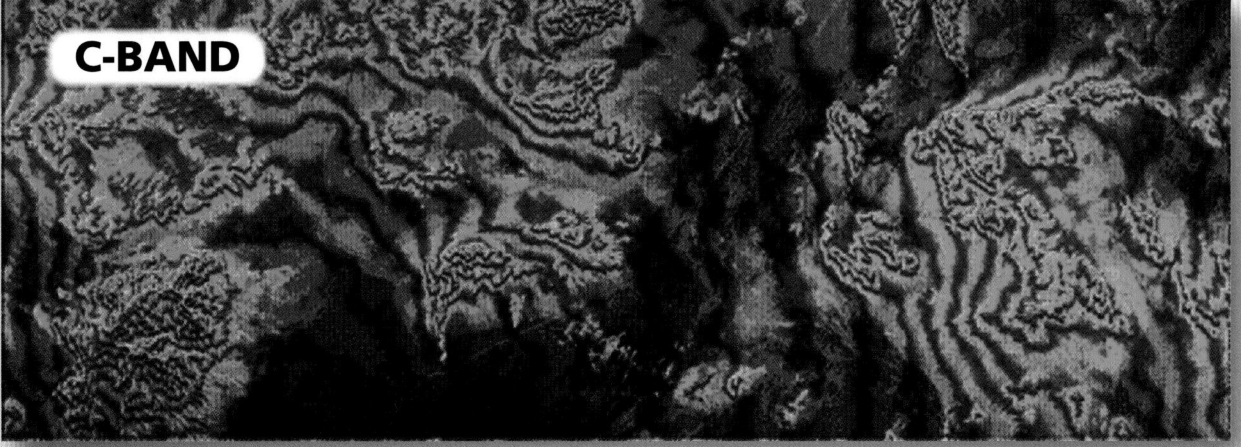

See page 50 for a map of France made using this data.

Shuttle radar topography mission (SRTM) sees the world. These three globes show the features of the world as seen from space in 3D.

This ongoing kind of project can map the whole world quickly. Successive mappings can show changes at comparatively low cost.

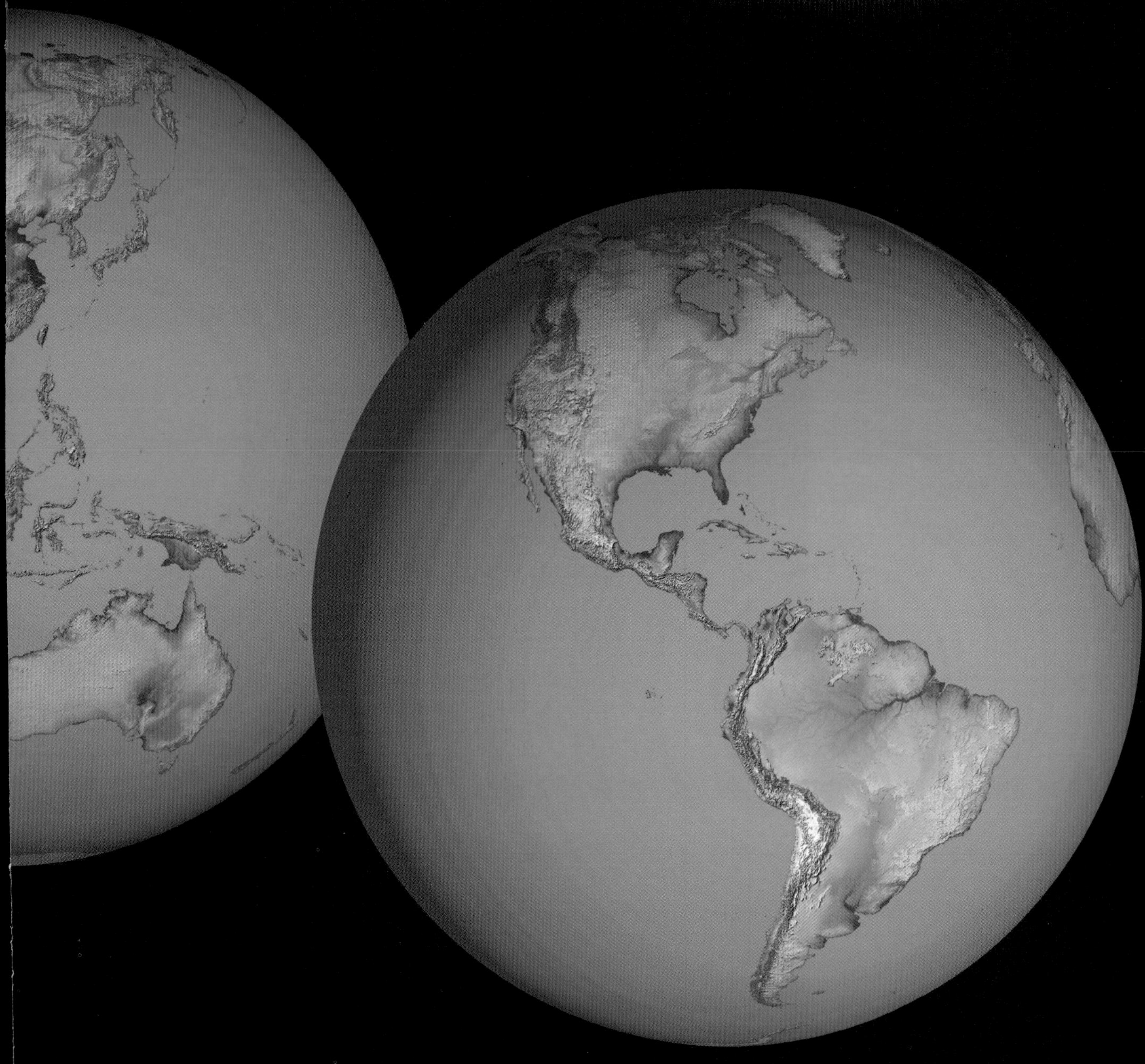

4: ASTRONOMICAL SATELLITES

Other pictures from astronomical telescopes can be found in Volume 1: *How the universe works* and Volume 2: *Sun and solar system.*

As we said earlier in this book, it is possible to use satellites to look "up" as well as "down." The satellites that look up are astronomical telescopes and sensors.

To see why satellites benefit **ASTRONOMY**, think of what you see in the night sky. Look up, and you see far more stars than if you look toward the horizon. The reason for this is that the amount of atmosphere you look through if you look straight up is far less than the amount you look through close to the horizon. Dust and gases all absorb and reflect light, and that is why we only see the brightest stars above us. If you were able to take away the dust, the sky would immediately appear to have more stars in it, which is why so many ground-based telescopes are on the tops of high mountains.

Look up again, and see the stars twinkling. They do not, of course, twinkle any more than our Sun varies. The effect you see is the result of air movements that are distorting the light reaching us. Again, remove the air, and these distortions can also be removed.

▲ In the center of this **HUBBLE SPACE TELESCOPE** image of the Large Magellanic Cloud, a nearby galaxy, there is a **SUPERNOVA** (1987A), or star explosion.

The many bright-blue stars near the supernova are massive young stars, while the presence of bright gas clouds is another sign of the youth and is a breeding ground for new stars.

▶ This is an image of a small portion of the Cygnus Loop supernova remnant, taken with the wide field planetary camera on the Hubble Space Telescope.

The Cygnus Loop marks the edge of a bubblelike, expanding blast wave from a colossal stellar explosion that occurred about 15,000 years ago.

ASTRONOMY The study of space beyond the Earth and its contents.

HUBBLE SPACE TELESCOPE An orbiting telescope (and so a satellite) that was placed above the Earth's atmosphere so that it could take images that were far clearer than anything that could be obtained from the surface of the Earth.

SUPERNOVA A violently exploding star that becomes millions or even billions of times brighter than when it was younger and stable.

▲▼ The Hubble Space Telescope.

The first astronomical satellites

As you can see, there are powerful reasons for using sensors and telescopes in space. The first satellites launched by the U.S. were called Explorer (see page 28). The first went up in 1958. By the end of the project in 1984, 65 satellites had been orbited. They were able to give us pictures of a wide range of phenomena, such as the **SOLAR WIND** and the Earth's **MAGNETIC FIELD.**

The Orbiting Solar Observatory (OSO), sent up in 1962, was the first of a series of observatories that point toward the Sun and record and transmit a variety of data about our star. Many others were to follow it, not just in Earth orbit but also in a solar, or halo, orbit, in which the Sun-Earth **GRAVITATIONAL FIELDS** are balanced.

The first **X-RAYS** from space were detected in 1962. Since then satellites have found X-ray sources in **BLACK HOLES**, **NEUTRON STARS**, and supernovas.

The Orbiting Astronomical Observatory (OAO) is a large satellite equipped with a stabilized guidance system and designed to map the entire sky. In 1968 OAO began exploring the universe using **ULTRAVIOLET** sensors. Sources of great intensity were soon discovered in supernovas and **QUASARS.**

Hubble Space Telescope

By far the most powerful telescope placed in orbit is the Hubble Space Telescope (HST), which was launched from the **SPACE SHUTTLE** in 1990. This telescope has a 2.4-meter primary mirror that can resolve (see) objects by a factor of ten better than from any ground-based observatory. One of its main uses is to look at **NEBULAS**, **GALAXIES**, and quasars.

The wide field planetary camera II on Hubble is able to detect objects as faint as the 28th **MAGNITUDE**, which is about a billionth as faint as can be seen with the naked eye.

Another Hubble camera is the faint object camera (FOC). It provides a higher resolution on objects of special interest. Hubble also contains the near infrared camera (NIC), the multiobject spectrometer (NICMOS), and the space telescope imaging spectrograph (STIS).

ANTENNA (pl. **ANTENNAE**) A device used for sending out and receiving radio waves.

BIG BANG The theory that the universe as we know it started from a single point (called a singularity) and then exploded outward. It is still expanding today.

BLACK HOLE An object that has a gravitational pull so strong that nothing can escape from it.

GALAXY A system of stars and interstellar matter within the universe.

GRAVITATIONAL FIELD The region surrounding a body in which that body's gravitational force can be felt.

MAGNETIC FIELD The region of influence of a magnetic body.

MAGNITUDE A measure of the brightness of a star.

MICROWAVE RADIATION The background radiation that is found everywhere in space, and whose existence is used to support the Big Bang theory.

NEBULA (pl. **NEBULAE**) Clouds of gas and dust that exist in the space between stars.

NEUTRON STAR A very dense star that consists only of tightly packed neutrons. It is the result of the collapse of a massive star.

QUASAR A rare starlike object of enormous brightness that gives out radio waves, which are thought to be released as material is sucked toward a black hole.

SOLAR PANELS Large flat surfaces covered with thousands of small photoelectric devices that convert solar radiation into electricity.

SOLAR WIND The flow of tiny charged particles (called plasma) outward from the Sun.

SPACE SHUTTLE NASA's reusable space vehicle that is launched like a rocket but returns like a glider.

ULTRAVIOLET A form of radiation that is just beyond the violet end of the visible spectrum and so is called "ultra" (more than) violet. At the other end of the visible spectrum is "infra" (less than) red.

X-RAY An invisible form of radiation that has extremely short wavelengths just beyond the ultraviolet.

In particular, NICMOS looks at the near infrared to provide information about the birth of a star.

The STIS is designed to obscure the light from stars so that black holes or large planets can be identified in other galaxies.

Other astronomical satellites

The Extreme Ultraviolet Explorer (EUE) was sent up in 1992, and it has now surveyed the entire sky.

At the other end of the visible spectrum the Infrared Astronomical Satellite (IRAS) was also launched. During its lifespan IRAS observed 20,000 galaxies, 130,000 stars, and 90,000 other space objects and star clusters.

Cosmic Background Explorer (COBE) is designed to study the physical conditions in the very early universe and the start of organization following the **BIG BANG**. It does so by measuring the diffuse infrared and **MICROWAVE RADIATION** from the early universe.

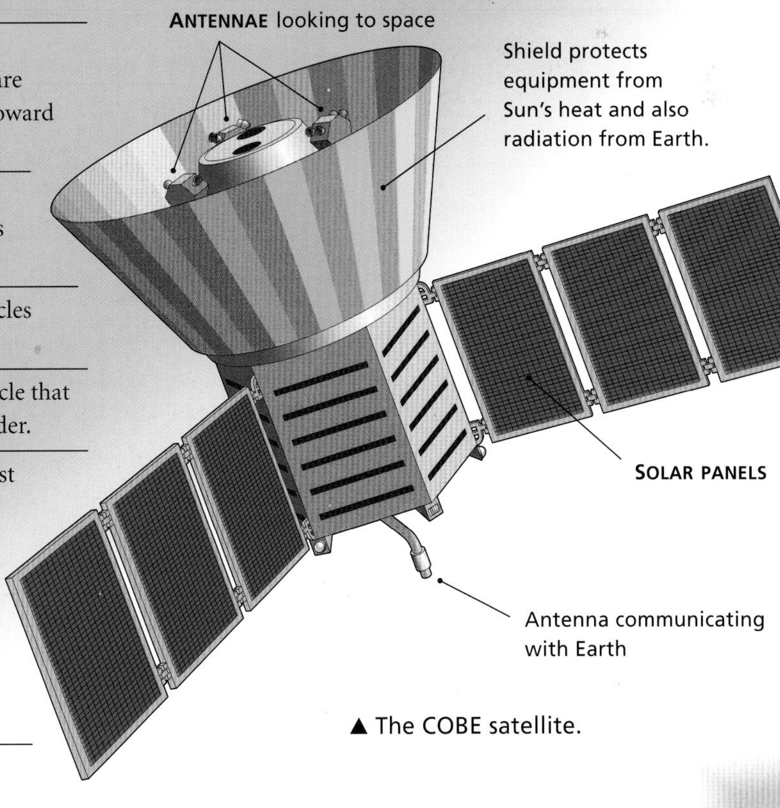

▲ The COBE satellite.

SET GLOSSARY

Metric (SI) and U.S. standard unit conversion table

1 kilometer = 0.6 mile
1 meter = 3.3 feet or 1.1 yards
1 centimeter = 0.4 inch
1 tonne = (metric ton) 1,000 kilograms, or 2,204.6 pounds
1 kilogram = 2.2 pounds
1 gram = 0.035 ounces

1 mile = 1.6 kilometers
1 foot = 0.3 meter
1 inch = 25.4 millimeters or 2.54 centimeters
1 ton = 907.18 kilograms in standard units, 1,016.05 kilograms in metric
1 pound = 0.45 kilograms
1 ounce = 28 grams

0°C = 5/9 (32°F)

ABSOLUTE ZERO The coldest possible temperature, defined as 0 K or –273°C.
See also: **K**.

ACCELERATE To gain speed.

AERODYNAMIC A shape offering as little resistance to the air as possible.

AIR RESISTANCE The frictional drag that an object creates as it moves rapidly through the air.

AMINO ACIDS Simple organic molecules that can be building blocks for living things.

ANNULAR Ringlike.
An annular eclipse occurs when the dark disk of the Moon does not completely obscure the Sun.

ANTENNA (pl. **ANTENNAE**) A device, often in the shape of a rod or wire, used for sending out and receiving radio waves.

ANTICLINE An arching fold of rock layers where the rocks slope down from the crest.

ANTICYCLONE A roughly circular region of the atmosphere that is spiraling outward and downward.

APOGEE The point on an orbit where the orbiting object is at its farthest from the object it is orbiting.

APOLLO The program developed in the United States by NASA to get people to the Moon's surface and back safely.

ARRAY A regular group or arrangement.

ASH Fragments of lava that have cooled and solidified between when they leave a volcano and when they fall to the surface.

ASTEROID Any of the many small objects within the solar system.
Asteroids are rocky or metallic and are conventionally described as significant bodies with a diameter smaller than 1,000 km. Asteroids mainly occupy a belt between Mars and Jupiter (asteroid belt).

ASTEROID BELT The collection of asteroids that orbit the Sun between the orbits of Mars and Jupiter.

ASTHENOSPHERE The region below the lithosphere, and therefore part of the upper mantle, in which some material may be molten.

ASTRONOMICAL UNIT (AU) The average distance from the Earth to the Sun (149,597,870 km).

ASTRONOMY The study of space beyond the Earth and its contents. It includes those phenomena that affect the Earth but that originate in space, such as meteorites and aurora.

ASTROPHYSICS The study of physics in space, what other stars, galaxies, and planets are like, and the physical laws that govern them.

ASYNCHRONOUS Not connected in time or pace.

ATMOSPHERE The envelope of gases that surrounds the Earth and other bodies in the universe.
The Earth's atmosphere is very different from that of other planets, being, for example, far lower in hydrogen and helium than the gas giants and lower in carbon dioxide than Venus, but richer in oxygen than all the others.

ATMOSPHERIC PRESSURE The pressure on the gases in the atmosphere caused by gravity pulling them toward the center of a celestial body.

ATOM The smallest particle of an element.

ATOMIC MASS UNIT A measure of the mass of an atom or molecule.
An atomic mass unit equals one-twelfth of the mass of an atom of carbon-12.

ATOMIC WEAPONS Weapons that rely on the violent explosive force achieved when radioactive materials are made to go into an uncontrollable chain reaction.

ATOMIC WEIGHT The ratio of the average mass of a chemical element's atoms to carbon-12.

AURORA A region of illumination, often in the form of a wavy curtain, high in the atmosphere of a planet.
It is the result of the interaction of the planet's magnetic field with the particles in the solar wind. High-energy electrons from the solar wind race along the planet's magnetic field into the upper atmosphere. The electrons excite atmospheric gases, making them glow.

AXIS (pl. **AXES**) The line around which a body spins.
The Earth spins around an axis through its north and south geographic poles.

BALLISTIC MISSILE A rocket that is guided up in a high arching path; then the fuel supply is cut, and it is allowed to fall to the ground.

BASIN A large depression in the ground (bigger than a crater).

BIG BANG The theory that the universe as we know it started from a single point (called a singularity) and then exploded outward. It is still expanding today.

BINARY STAR A pair of stars that are gravitationally attracted, and that revolve around one another.

BLACK DWARF A degenerate star that has cooled so that it is now not visible.

BLACK HOLE An object that has a gravitational pull so strong that nothing can escape from it.
A black hole may have a mass equal to thousands of stars or more.

BLUE GIANT A young, extremely bright and hot star of very large mass that has used up all its hydrogen and is no longer in the main sequence. When a blue giant ages, it becomes a red giant.

BOILING POINT The change of state of a substance in which a liquid rapidly turns into a gas without a change in temperature.

BOOSTER POD A form of housing that stands outside the main body of the launcher.

CALDERA A large pit in the top of a volcano produced when the top of the volcano explodes and collapses in on itself.

CAPSULE A small pressurized space vehicle.

CATALYST A substance that speeds up a chemical reaction but that is itself unchanged.

CELESTIAL Relating to the sky above, the "heavens."

CENTER OF GRAVITY The point at which all of the mass of an object can be balanced.

CENTRIFUGAL FORCE A force that acts on an orbiting or spinning body, tending to oppose gravity and move away from the center of rotation.
For orbiting objects the centrifugal force acts in the opposite direction from gravity. When satellites orbit the Earth, the centrifugal force balances out the force of gravity.

CENTRIFUGE An instrument for spinning small samples very rapidly.

CHAIN REACTION A sequence of related events with one event triggering the next.

CHASM A deep, narrow trench.

CHROMOSPHERE The shell of gases that makes up part of the atmosphere of a star and lies between the photosphere and the corona.

CIRCUMFERENCE The distance around the edge of a circle or sphere.

COMA The blurred image caused by light bouncing from a collection of dust and ice particles escaping from the nucleus of a comet.

The coma changes the appearance of a comet from a point source of reflective light to a blurry object with a tail.

COMBUSTION CHAMBER A vessel inside an engine or motor where the fuel components mix and are set on fire, that is, they are burned (combusted).

COMET A small object, often described as being like a dirty snowball, that appears to be very bright in the night sky and has a long tail when it approaches the Sun.

Comets are thought to be some of the oldest objects in the solar system.

COMPLEMENTARY COLOR A color that is diametrically opposed in the range, or circle, of colors in the spectrum; for example, cyan (blue) is the complement of red.

COMPOSITE A material made from solid threads in a liquid matrix that is allowed to set.

COMPOUND A substance made from two or more elements that have chemically combined.

Ammonia is an example of a compound made from the elements hydrogen and nitrogen.

CONDENSE/CONDENSATION (1) To make something more concentrated or compact.

(2) The change of state from a gas or vapor to a liquid.

CONDUCTION The transfer of heat between two objects when they touch.

CONSTELLATION One of many commonly recognized patterns of stars in the sky.

CONVECTION/CONVECTION CURRENTS The circulating flow in a fluid (liquid or gas) that occurs when it is heated from below.

Convective flow is caused in a fluid by the tendency for hotter, and therefore less dense, material to rise and for colder, and therefore more dense, material, to sink with gravity. That results in a heat transfer.

CORE The central region of a body.

The core of the Earth is about 3,300 km in radius, compared with the radius of the whole Earth, which is 6,300 km.

CORONA (pl. **CORONAE**) (1) A colored circle seen around a bright object such as a star.

(2) The gases surrounding a star such as the Sun. In the case of the Sun and certain other stars these gases are extremely hot.

(3) A circular to oval pattern of faults, fractures, and ridges with a sagging center as found on Venus. In the case of Venus they are a few hundred kilometers in diameter.

CORONAL MASS EJECTIONS Very large bubbles of plasma escaping into the corona.

CORROSIVE SUBSTANCE Something that chemically eats away something else.

COSMOLOGICAL PRINCIPLE States that the way you see the universe is independent of the place where you are (your location). In effect, it means that the universe is roughly uniform throughout.

COSMONAUT A Russian space person.

COSMOS The universe and everything in it. The word "cosmos" suggests that the universe operates according to orderly principles.

CRATER A deep bowl-shaped depression in the surface of a body formed by the high-speed impact of another, smaller body.

Most craters are formed by the impact of asteroids and meteoroids. Craters have both a depression, or pit, and also an elevated rim formed of the material displaced from the central pit.

CRESCENT The appearance of the Moon when it is between a new Moon and a half Moon.

CRUST The solid outer surface of a rocky body.

The crust of the Earth is mainly just a few tens of kilometers thick, compared to the total radius of 6,300 km for the whole Earth. It forms much of the lithosphere.

CRYSTAL An ordered arrangement of molecules in a compound. Crystals that grow freely develop flat surfaces.

CYCLONE A large storm in which the atmosphere spirals inward and upward.

On Earth cyclones have a very low atmospheric pressure at their center and often contain deep clouds.

DARK MATTER Matter that does not shine or reflect light.

No one has ever found dark matter, but it is thought to exist because the amount of ordinary matter in the universe is not enough to account for many gravitational effects that have been observed.

DENSITY A measure of the amount of matter in a space.

Density is often measured in grams per cubic centimeter. The density of the Earth is 5.5 grams per cubic centimeter.

DEORBIT To move out of an orbital position and begin a reentry path toward the Earth.

DEPRESSION (1) A sunken area or hollow in a surface or landscape.

(2) A region of inward swirling air in the atmosphere associated with cloudy weather and rain.

DIFFRACTION The bending of light as it goes through materials of different density.

DISK A shape or surface that looks round and flat.

DOCK To meet with and attach to another space vehicle.

DOCKING PORT/STATION A place on the side of a spacecraft that contains some form of anchoring mechanism and an airlock.

DOPPLER EFFECT The apparent change in pitch of a fast-moving object as it approaches or leaves an observer.

DOWNLINK A communication to Earth from a spacecraft.

DRAG A force that hinders the movement of something.

DWARF STAR A star that shines with a brightness that is average or below.

EARTH The third planet from the Sun and the one on which we live.

The Earth belongs to the group of rocky planets. It is unique in having an oxygen-rich atmosphere and water, commonly found in its three phases—solid, liquid, and gas.

EARTHQUAKE The shock waves produced by the sudden movement of two pieces of brittle crust.

ECCENTRIC A noncircular, or oval, orbit.

ECLIPSE The time when light is cut off by a body coming between the observer and the source of the illumination (for example, eclipse of the Sun), or when the body the observer is on comes between the source of illumination and another body (for example, eclipse of the Moon).

It happens when three bodies are in a line. This phenomenon is not necessarily called an eclipse. Occultations of stars by the Moon and transits of Venus or Mercury are examples of different expressions used instead of "eclipse."

See also: **TOTAL ECLIPSE.**

ECOLOGY The study of living things in their environment.

ELECTRONS Negatively charged particles that are parts of atoms.

ELEMENT A substance that cannot be decomposed into simpler substances by chemical means.

Elements are the building blocks of compounds. For example, silicon and oxygen are elements. They combine to form the compound silicon dioxide, or quartz.

ELLIPTICAL GALAXY A galaxy that has an oval shape rather like a football, and that has no spiral arms.

EL NIÑO A time when ocean currents in the Pacific Ocean reverse from their normal pattern and disrupt global weather patterns. It occurs once every 4 or 5 years.

EMISSION Something that is sent or let out.

ENCKE GAP A gap between rings around Saturn named for the astronomer Johann Franz Encke (1791–1865).

EPOXY RESIN Adhesives that develop their strength as they react, or "cure," after mixing.

EQUATOR The ring drawn around a body midway between the poles.

EQUILIBRIUM A state of balance.

ESA The European Space Agency. ESA is an organizaton of European countries for cooperation in space research and technology. It operates several installations around Europe and has its headquarters in Paris, France.

ESCARPMENT A sharp-edged ridge.

EVAPORATE/EVAPORATION The change in state from liquid to a gas.

EXOSPHERE The outer part of the atmosphere starting about 500 km from the surface. This layer contains so little air that molecules rarely collide.

EXTRAVEHICULAR ACTIVITY Any task performed by people outside the protected environment of a space vehicle's pressurized compartments. Extravehicular activities (EVA) include repairing equipment in the Space Shuttle bay.

FALSE COLOR The colors used to make the appearance of some property more obvious.

They are part of the computer generation of an image.

FAULT A place in the crust where rocks have fractured, and then one side has moved relative to the other.

A fault is caused by excessive pressure on brittle rocks.

FLUORESCENT Emitting the visible light produced by a substance when it is struck by invisible waves, such as ultraviolet waves.

FRACTURE A break in brittle rock.

FREQUENCY The number of complete cycles of (for example, radio) waves received per second.

FRICTION The force that resists two bodies that are in contact.

For example, the effect of the ocean waters moving as tides slows the Earth's rotation.

FUSION The joining of atomic nuclei to form heavier nuclei.

This process results in the release of huge amounts of energy.

GALAXY A system of stars and interstellar matter within the universe.

Galaxies may contain billions of stars.

GALILEAN SATELLITES The four large satellites of Jupiter discovered by astronomer Galileo Galilei in 1610. They are Callisto, Europa, Ganymede, and Io.

GALILEO A U.S. space probe launched in October 1989 and designed for intensive investigation of Jupiter.

GEIGER TUBE A device to detect radioactive materials.

GEOSTATIONARY ORBIT A circular orbit 35,786 km directly above the Earth's equator.

Communications satellites frequently use this orbit. A satellite in a geostationary orbit will move at the same rate as the Earth's rotation, completing one revolution in 24 hours. That way it remains at the same point over the Earth's equator.

GEOSTATIONARY SATELLITE A man-made satellite in a fixed or geosynchronous orbit around the Earth.

GEOSYNCHRONOUS ORBIT An orbit in which a satellite makes one circuit of the Earth in 24 hours.

A geosynchronous orbit coincides with the Earth's orbit—it takes the same time to complete an orbit as it does for the Earth to make one complete rotation. If the orbit is circular and above the equator, then the satellite remains over one particular point of the equator; that is called a geostationary orbit.

GEOSYNCLINE A large downward sag or trench that forms in the Earth's crust as a result of colliding tectonic plates.

GEYSER A periodic fountain of material. On Earth geysers are of water and steam, but on other planets and moons they are formed from other substances, for example, nitrogen gas on Triton.

GIBBOUS When between half and a full disk of a body can be seen lighted by the Sun.

GIMBALS A framework that allows anything inside it to move in a variety of directions.

GLOBAL POSITIONING SYSTEM A network of geostationary satellites that can be used to locate the position of any object on the Earth's surface.

GRANULATION The speckled pattern we see in the Sun's photosphere as a result of convectional overturning of gases.

GRAVITATIONAL FIELD The region surrounding a body in which that body's gravitational force can be felt.

The gravitational field of the Sun spreads over the entire solar system. The gravitational fields of the planets each exert some influence on the orbits of their neighbors.

GRAVITY/GRAVITATIONAL FORCE/ GRAVITATIONAL PULL The force of attraction between bodies. The larger an object, the more its gravitational pull on other objects.

The Sun's gravity is the most powerful in the solar system, keeping all of the planets and other materials within the solar system.

GREAT RED SPOT A large, almost permanent feature of the Jovian atmosphere that moves around the planet at about latitude 23°S.

GREENHOUSE EFFECT The increase in atmospheric temperature produced by the presence of carbon dioxide in the air.

Carbon dioxide has the ability to soak up heat radiated from the surface of a planet and partly prevent its escape. The effect is similar to that produced by a greenhouse.

GROUND STATION A receiving and transmitting station in direct communication with satellites. Such stations are characterized by having large dish-shaped antennae.

GULLY (pl. **GULLIES**) A trench in the land surface formed, on Earth, by running water.

GYROSCOPE A device in which a rapidly spinning wheel is held in a frame in such a way that it can rotate in any direction. The momentum of the wheel means that the gyroscope retains its position even when the frame is tilted.

HEAT SHIELD A protective device on the outside of a space vehicle that absorbs the heat during reentry and protects it from burning up.

HELIOPAUSE The edge of the heliosphere.

HELIOSEISMOLOGY The study of the internal structure of the Sun by modeling the Sun's patterns of internal shock waves.

HELIOSPHERE The entire range of influence of the Sun. It extends to the edge of the solar system.

HUBBLE SPACE TELESCOPE An orbiting telescope (and so a satellite) that was placed above the Earth's atmosphere so that it could take images that were far clearer than anything that could be obtained from the surface of the Earth.

HURRICANE A very violent cyclone that begins close to the equator, and that contains winds of over 117 km/hr.

ICE CAP A small mountainous region that is covered in ice.

INFRARED Radiation with a wavelength that is longer than red light.

INNER PLANETS The rocky planets closest to the Sun. They are Mercury, Venus, Earth, and Mars.

INTERNATIONAL SPACE STATION The international orbiting space laboratory.

INTERPLANETARY DUST The fine dustlike material that lies scattered through space, and that exists between the planets as well as in outer space.

INTERSTELLAR Between the stars.

IONIZED Matter that has been converted into small charged particles called ions.

An atom that has gained or lost an electron.

IONOSPHERE A part of the Earth's atmosphere in which the number of ions (electrically charged particles) is enough to affect how radio waves move.

The ionosphere begins about 50 km above the Earth's surface.

IRREGULAR SATELLITES Satellites that orbit in the opposite direction from their parent planet.

This motion is also called retrograde rotation.

ISOTOPE Atoms that have the same number of protons in their nucleus, but that have different masses; for example, carbon-12 and carbon-14.

JOVIAN PLANETS An alternative group name for the gas giant planets: Jupiter, Saturn, Uranus, and Neptune.

JUPITER The fifth planet from the Sun and two planets farther away from the Sun than the Earth.

Jupiter is 318 times as massive as the Earth and 1,500 times as big by volume. It is the largest of the gas giants.

K Named for British scientist Lord Kelvin (1824–1907), it is a measurement of absolute temperature. Zero K is called absolute zero and is only approached in deep space: ice melts at 273 K, and water boils at 373 K.

KEELER GAP A gap in the rings of Saturn named for the astronomer James Edward Keeler (1857–1900).

KILOPARSEC A unit of a thousand parsecs. A parsec is the unit used for measuring the largest distances in the universe.

KUIPER BELT A belt of planetesimals (small rocky bodies, one kilometer to hundreds of kilometers across) much closer to the Sun than the Oort cloud.

LANDSLIDE A sudden collapse of material on a steep slope.

LA NIÑA Below normal ocean temperatures in the eastern Pacific Ocean that disrupt global weather patterns.

LATITUDE Angular distance north or south of the equator, measured through 90°.

LAUNCH VEHICLE/LAUNCHER A system of propellant tanks and rocket motors or engines designed to lift a payload into space. It may, or may not, be part of a space vehicle.

LAVA Hot, melted rock from a volcano.

Lava flows onto the surface of a planet and cools and hardens to form new rock. Most of the lava on Earth is made of basalt.

LAVA FLOW A river or sheet of liquid volcanic rock.

LAWS OF MOTION Formulated by Sir Isaac Newton, they describe the forces that act on a moving object.

The first law states that an object will keep moving in a straight line at constant speed unless it is acted on by a force.

The second law states that the force on an object is related to the mass of the object multiplied by its acceleration.

The third law states that an action always has an equal and directly opposite reaction.

LIFT An upthrust on the wing of a plane that occurs when it moves rapidly through the air. It is the main way of suspending an airplane during flight. The engines simply provide the forward thrust.

LIGHT-YEAR The distance traveled by light through space in one Earth year, or 63,240 astronomical units.

The speed of light is the speed that light travels through a vacuum, which is 299,792 km/s.

LIMB The outer edge of a celestial body, including an atmosphere if it has one.

LITHOSPHERE The upper part of the Earth, corresponding generally to the crust and believed to be about 80 km thick.

LOCAL GROUP The Milky Way, the Magellanic Clouds, the Andromeda Galaxy, and over 20 other relatively near galaxies.

LUNAR Anything to do with the Moon.

MAGELLANIC CLOUD Either of two small galaxies that are companions to the Milky Way Galaxy.

MAGMA Hot, melted rock inside the Earth that, when cooled, forms igneous rock.

Magma is associated with volcanic activity.

MAGNETIC FIELD The region of influence of a magnetic body.

The Earth's magnetic field stretches out beyond the atmosphere into space. There it interacts with the solar wind to produce auroras.

MAGNETISM An invisible force that has the property of attracting iron and similar metals.

MAGNETOPAUSE The outer edge of the magnetosphere.

MAGNETOSPHERE A region in the upper atmosphere, or around a planet, where magnetic phenomena such as auroras are found.

MAGNITUDE A measure of the brightness of a star.

The apparent magnitude is the brightness of a celestial object as seen from the Earth. The absolute magnitude is the standardized brightness measured as though all objects were the same distance from the Earth. The brighter the object, the lower its magnitude number. For example, a star of magnitude 4 is 2.5 times as bright as one of magnitude 5. A difference of five magnitudes is the same as a difference in brightness of 100 to 1. The brightest stars have negative numbers. The Sun's apparent magnitude is –26.8. Its absolute magnitude is 4.8.

MAIN SEQUENCE The 90% of stars in the universe that represent the mature phase of stars with small or medium mass.

MANTLE The region of a planet between the core and the crust.

The Earth's mantle is about 2,900 km thick, and its upper surface may be molten in some places.

MARE (pl. **MARIA**) A flat, dark plain created by lava flows. They were once thought to be seas.

MARS The fourth planet from the Sun in our solar system and one planet farther away from the Sun than the Earth.

Mars is a rocky planet almost half the diameter of Earth that is a distinctive rust-red color.

MASCON A region of higher surface density on the Moon.

MASS The amount of matter in an object.

The amount of matter, and so the mass, remains the same, but the effect of gravity gives the mass a weight. The weight depends on the gravitational pull. Thus a ball will have the same mass on the Earth and on the Moon, but it will weigh a sixth as much on the Moon because the force of gravity there is only a sixth as strong.

MATTER Anything that exists in physical form.

Everything we can see is made of matter. The building blocks of matter are atoms.

MERCURY The closest planet to the Sun in our solar system and two planets closer to the Sun than Earth.

Mercury is a gray-colored rocky planet less than half the diameter of Earth. It has the most extreme temperature range of any planet in our solar system.

MESOSPHERE One of the upper regions of the atmosphere, beginning at the top of the stratosphere and continuing from 50 km upward until the temperature stops declining.

METEOR A streak of light (shooting star) produced by a meteoroid as it enters the Earth's atmosphere.

The friction with the Earth's atmosphere causes the small body to glow (become incandescent). That is what we see as a streak of light.

METEORITE A meteor that reaches the Earth's surface.

METEOROID A small body moving in the solar system that becomes a meteor if it enters the Earth's atmosphere.

Meteoroids are typically only a few millimeters across and burn up as they go through the atmosphere, but some have crashed to the Earth, making large craters.

MICROMETEORITES Tiny pieces of space dust moving at high speeds.

MICRON A millionth of a meter.

MICROWAVELENGTH Waves at the shortest end of the radio wavelengths.

MICROWAVE RADIATION The background radiation that is found everywhere in space, and whose existence is used to support the Big Bang theory.

MILKY WAY The spiral galaxy in which our star and solar system are situated.

MINERAL A solid crystalline substance.

MINOR PLANET Another term for an asteroid.

M NUMBER In 1781 Charles Messier began a catalogue of the objects he could see in the night sky. He gave each of them a unique number. The first entry was called M1. There is no significance to the number in terms of brightness, size, closeness, or otherwise.

MODULE A section, or part, of a space vehicle.

MOLECULE A group of two or more atoms held together by chemical bonds.

MOLTEN Liquid, suggesting that it has changed from a solid.

MOMENTUM The mass of an object multiplied by its velocity.

MOON The natural satellite that orbits the Earth.

Other planets have large satellites, or moons, but none is relatively as large as our Moon, suggesting that it has a unique origin.

MOON The name generally given to any large natural satellite of a planet.

MOUNTAIN RANGE A long, narrow region of very high land that contains several or many mountains.

NASA The National Aeronautics and Space Administration.

NASA was founded in 1958 for aeronautical and space exploration. It operates several installations around the country and has its headquarters in Washington, D.C.

NEAP TIDE A tide showing the smallest difference between high and low tides.

NEBULA (pl. **NEBULAE**) Clouds of gas and dust that exist in the space between stars.

The word means mist or cloud and is also used as an alternative to galaxy. The gas makes up to 5% of the mass of a galaxy. What a nebula looks like depends on the arrangement of gas and dust within it.

NEPTUNE The eighth planet from the Sun in our solar system and five planets farther away from the Sun than the Earth.

Neptune is a gas planet that is almost four times the diameter of Earth. It is blue.

NEUTRINOS An uncharged fundamental particle that is thought to have no mass.

NEUTRONS Particles inside the core of an atom that are neutral (have no charge).

NEUTRON STAR A very dense star that consists only of tightly packed neutrons. It is the result of the collapse of a massive star.

NOBLE GASES The unreactive gases, such as neon, xenon, and krypton.

NOVA (pl. **NOVAE**) (1) A star that suddenly becomes much brighter, then fades away to its original brightness within a few months. *See also:* **SUPERNOVA**.

(2) A radiating pattern of faults and fractures unique to Venus.

NUCLEAR DEVICES Anything that is powered by a source of radioactivity.

NUCLEUS (pl. **NUCLEI**) The centermost part of something, the core.

OORT CLOUD A region on the edge of the solar system that consists of planetesimals and comets that did not get caught up in planet making.

OPTICAL Relating to the use of light.

ORBIT The path followed by one object as it tracks around another.

The orbits of the planets around the Sun and moons around their planets are oval, or elliptical.

ORGANIC MATERIAL Any matter that contains carbon and is alive.

OUTER PLANETS The gas giant planets Jupiter, Saturn, Uranus, and Neptune plus the rocky planet Pluto.

OXIDIZER The substance in a reaction that removes electrons from and thereby oxidizes (burns) another substance.

In the case of oxygen this results in the other substance combining with the oxygen to form an oxide (also called an oxidizing agent).

OZONE A form of oxygen (O_3) with three atoms in each molecule instead of the more usual two (O_2).

OZONE HOLE The observed lack of the gas ozone in the upper atmosphere.

PARSEC The unit used for measuring the largest distances in the universe.

A parsec is the distance at which an observer in space would see the radius of the orbit as making one second of arc. This gives a distance of about 3.26 light-years.

See also: **KILOPARSEC**.

PAYLOAD The spacecraft that is carried into space by a launcher.

PENUMBRA (1) A region that is in semidarkness during an eclipse.

(2) The part of a sunspot surrounding the umbra.

PERCOLATE To flow by gravity between particles, for example, of soil.

PERIGEE The point on an orbit where the orbiting object is as close as it ever comes to the object it is orbiting.

PHARMACEUTICAL Relating to medicinal drugs.

PHASE The differing appearance of a body that is closer to the Sun, and that is illuminated by it.

PHOTOCHEMICAL SMOG A hazy atmosphere, often brown, resulting from the reaction of nitrogen gases with sunlight.

PHOTOMOSAIC A composite picture made up of several other pictures that individually only cover a small area.

PHOTON A particle (quantum) of electromagnetic radiation.

PHOTOSPHERE A shell of the Sun that we regard as its visible surface.

PHOTOSYNTHESIS The process that plants use to combine the substances in the environment, such as carbon dioxide, minerals, and water, with oxygen and energy-rich organic compounds by using the energy of sunlight.

PIONEER A name for a series of unmanned U.S. spacecraft.

Pioneer 1 was launched into lunar orbit on October 11, 1958. The others all went into deep space.

PLAIN A flat or gently rolling part of a landscape.

Plains are confined to lowlands. If a flat surface exists in an upland, it is called a plateau.

PLANE A flat surface.

PLANET Any of the large bodies that orbit the Sun.

The planets are (outward from the Sun): Mercury, Venus, Earth, Mars, Jupiter, Saturn, Uranus, Neptune, and Pluto. The rocky planets all have densities greater than 3 grams per cubic centimeter; the gaseous ones less than 2 grams per cubic centimeter.

PLANETARY NEBULA A compact ring or oval nebula that is made of material thrown out of a hot star.

The term "planetary nebula" is a misnomer; dying stars create these cocoons when they lose outer layers of gas. The process has nothing to do with planet formation, which is predicted to happen early in a star's life.

The term originates from a time when people, looking through weak telescopes, thought that the nebulae resembled planets within the solar system, when in fact they were expanding shells of glowing gas in far-off galaxies.

PLANETESIMAL Small rocky bodies one kilometer to hundreds of kilometers across.

The word especially relates to materials that exist in the early stages of the formation of a star and its planets from the dust of a nebula, which will eventually group together to form planets. Some are rock, others a mixture of rock and ice.

PLANKTON Microscopic creatures that float in water.

PLASMA A collection of charged particles that behaves something like a gas. It can conduct an electric charge and be affected by magnetic fields.

PLASTIC The ability of certain solid substances to be molded or deformed to a new shape under pressure without cracking.

PLATE A very large unbroken part of the crust of a planet. Also called tectonic plate.

On Earth the tectonic plates are dragged across the surface by convection currents in the underlying mantle.

PLATEAU An upland plain or tableland.

PLUTO The ninth planet from the Sun and six planets farther from the Sun than the Earth.

Pluto is one of the rocky planets, but it is very different from the others, perhaps being a mixture of rock and ice. It is about two-thirds the size of our Moon.

POLE The geographic pole is the place where a line drawn along the axis of rotation exits from a body's surface.

Magnetic poles do not always correspond with geographic poles.

POLYMER A compound that is made up of long chains formed by combining molecules called monomers as repeating units. ("Poly" means many, "mer" means part.)

PRESSURE The force per unit area.

PROBE An unmanned spacecraft designed to explore our solar system and beyond.

Voyager, Cassini, and Magellan are examples of probes.

PROJECTILE An object propelled through the air or space by an external force or an on-board engine.

PROMINENCE A cloud of burning ionized gas that rises through the Sun's chromosphere into the corona. It can take the form of a sheet or a loop.

PROPELLANT A gas, liquid, or solid that can be expelled rapidly from the end of an object in order to give it motion.

Liquefied gases and solids are used as rocket propellants.

PROPULSION SYSTEM The motors or rockets and their tanks designed to give a launcher or space vehicle the thrust it needs.

PROTEIN Molecules in living things that are vital for building tissues.

PROTONS Positively charged particles from the core of an atom.

PROTOSTAR A cloud of gas and dust that begins to swirl around; the resulting gravity gives birth to a star.

PULSAR A neutron star that is spinning around, releasing electromagnetic radiation, including radio waves.

QUANTUM THEORY A concept of how energy can be divided into tiny pieces called quanta, which is the key to how the smallest particles work and how they build together to make the universe around us.

QUASAR A rare starlike object of enormous brightness that gives out radio waves, which are thought to be released as material is sucked toward a black hole.

RADAR Short for radio detecting and ranging. A system of bouncing radio waves from objects in order to map their surfaces and find out how far away they are.

Radar is useful in conditions where visible light cannot be used.

RADIATION/RADIATE The transfer of energy in the form of waves (such as light and heat) or particles (such as from radioactive decay of a material).

RADIOACTIVE/RADIOACTIVITY The property of some materials that emit radiation or energetic particles from the nucleus of their atoms.

RADIOACTIVE DECAY The change that takes place inside radioactive materials and causes them to give out progressively less radiation over time.

RADIO GALAXY A galaxy that gives out radio waves of enormous power.

RADIO INTERFERENCE Reduction in the radio communication effectiveness of the ionosphere caused by sunspots and other increases in the solar wind.

RADIO TELESCOPE A telescope that is designed to detect radio waves rather than light waves.

RADIO WAVES A form of electromagnetic radiation, like light and heat. Radio waves have a longer wavelength than light waves.

RADIUS (pl. **RADII**) The distance from the center to the outside of a circle or sphere.

RAY A line across the surface of a planet or moon made by material from a crater being flung across the surface.

REACTION An opposition to a force.

REACTIVE The ability of a chemical substance to combine readily with other substances. Oxygen is an example of a reactive substance.

RED GIANT A cool, large, bright star at least 25 times the diameter of our Sun.

REFLECT/REFLECTION/REFLECTIVE To bounce back any light that falls on a surface.

REGULAR SATELLITES Satellites that orbit in the same direction as their parent planet. This motion is also called synchronous rotation.

RESOLVING POWER The ability of an optical telescope to form an image of a distant object.

RETROGRADE DIRECTION An orbit the opposite of normal—that is, a planet that spins so the Sun rises in the west and sinks in the east.

RETROROCKET A rocket that fires against the direction of travel in order to slow down a space vehicle.

RIDGE A narrow crest of an upland area.

RIFT A trench made by the sinking of a part of the crust between parallel faults.

RIFT VALLEY A long trench in the surface of a planet produced by the collapse of the crust in a narrow zone.

ROCKET Any kind of device that uses the principle of jet propulsion, that is, the rapid release of gases designed to propel an object rapidly.

The word is also applied loosely to fireworks and spacecraft launch vehicles.

ROCKET ENGINE A propulsion system that burns liquid fuel such as liquid hydrogen.

ROCKET MOTOR A propulsion system that burns solid fuel such as hydrazine.

ROCKETRY Experimentation with rockets.

ROTATION Spinning around an axis.

SAND DUNE An aerodynamically shaped hump of sand.

SAROS CYCLE The interval of 18 years $11^{1}/_{3}$ days needed for the Earth, Sun, and Moon to come back into the same relative positions. It controls the pattern of eclipses.

SATELLITE (1) An object that is in an orbit around another object, usually a planet.

The Moon is a satellite of the Earth.

See also: **IRREGULAR SATELLITE, MOON, GALILEAN SATELLITE, REGULAR SATELLITE, SHEPHERD SATELLITE.**

(2) A man-made object that orbits the Earth. Usually used as a term for an unmanned spacecraft whose job is to acquire or transfer data to and from the ground.

SATURN The sixth planet from the Sun and three planets farther away from the Sun than the Earth.

It is the least-dense planet in the solar system, having 95 times the mass of the Earth, but 766 times the volume. It is one of the gas giant planets.

SCARP The steep slope of a sharp-crested ridge.

SEASONS The characteristic cycle of events in the heating of the Earth that causes related changes in weather patterns.

SEDIMENT Any particles of material that settle out, usually in layers, from a moving fluid such as air or water.

SEDIMENTARY Rocks deposited in layers.

SEISMIC Shaking, relating to earthquakes.

SENSOR A device used to detect something. Your eyes, ears, and nose are all sensors. Satellites use sensors that mainly detect changes in radio and other waves, including sunlight.

SHEPHERD SATELLITES Larger natural satellites that have an influence on small debris in nearby rings because of their gravity.

SHIELD VOLCANO A volcanic cone that is broad and gently sloping.

SIDEREAL MONTH The average time that the Moon takes to return to the same position against the background of stars.

SILT Particles with a range of 2 microns to 60 microns across.

SLINGSHOT TRAJECTORY A path chosen to use the attractive force of gravity to increase the speed of a spacecraft.

The craft is flown toward the planet or star, and it speeds up under the gravitational force. At the correct moment the path is taken to send the spacecraft into orbit and, when pointing in the right direction, to turn it from orbit, with its increased velocity, toward the final destination.

SOLAR Anything to do with the Sun.

SOLAR CELL A photoelectric device that converts the energy from the Sun (solar radiation) into electrical energy.

SOLAR FLARE Any sudden explosion from the surface of the Sun that sends ultraviolet radiation into the chromosphere. It also sends out some particles that reach Earth and disrupt radio communications.

SOLAR PANELS Large flat surfaces covered with thousands of small photoelectric devices that convert solar radiation into electricity.

SOLAR RADIATION The light and heat energy sent into space from the Sun.

Visible light and heat are just two of the many forms of energy sent by the Sun to the Earth.

SOLAR SYSTEM The Sun and the bodies orbiting around it.

The solar system contains nine major planets, at least 60 moons (large natural satellites), and a vast number of asteroids and comets, together with the gases within the system.

SOLAR WIND The flow of tiny charged particles (called plasma) outward from the Sun.

The solar wind stretches out across the solar system.

SONIC BOOM The noise created when an object moves faster than the speed of sound.

SPACE Everything beyond the Earth's atmosphere.

The word "space" is used rather generally. It can be divided up into inner space—the solar system, and outer space—everything beyond the solar system, for example, interstellar space.

SPACECRAFT Anything capable of moving beyond the Earth's atmosphere. Spacecraft can be manned or unmanned. Unmanned spacecraft are often referred to as space probes if they are exploring new areas.

SPACE RACE The period from the 1950s to the 1970s when the United States and the Soviet Union competed to be first in achievements in space.

SPACE SHUTTLE NASA's reusable space vehicle that is launched like a rocket but returns like a glider.

SPACE STATION A large man-made satellite used as a base for operations in space.

SPEED OF LIGHT *See:* **LIGHT-YEAR.**

SPHERE A ball-shaped object.

SPICULES Jets of relatively cool gas that move upward through the chromosphere into the corona.

SPIRAL GALAXY A galaxy that has a core of stars at the center of long curved arms made of even more stars arranged in a spiral shape.

SPRING TIDE A tide showing the greatest difference between high and low tides.

STAR A large ball of gases that radiates light. The star nearest the Earth is the Sun.

There are enormous numbers of stars in the universe, but few can be seen with the naked eye. Stars may occur singly, as our Sun, or in groups, of which pairs are most common.

STAR CLUSTER A group of gravitationally connected stars.

STELLAR WIND The flow of tiny charged particles (called plasma) outward from a star.

In our solar system the stellar wind is the same as the solar wind.

STRATOSPHERE The region immediately above the troposphere where the temperature increases with height, and the air is always stable.

It acts like an invisible lid, keeping the clouds in the troposphere.

SUBDUCTION ZONES Long, relatively thin, but very deep regions of the crust where one plate moves down and under, or subducts, another. They are the source of mountain ranges.

SUN The star that the planets of the solar system revolve around.

The Sun is 150 million km from the Earth and provides energy (in the form of light and heat) to our planet. Its density of 1.4 grams per cubic centimeter is similar to that of a gas giant planet.

SUNSPOT A spiral of gas found on the Sun that is moving slowly upward, and that is cooler than the surrounding gas and so looks darker.

SUPERNOVA A violently exploding star that becomes millions or even billions of times brighter than when it was younger and stable.

See also: **NOVA.**

SYNCHRONOUS Taking place at the same time.

SYNCHRONOUS ORBIT An orbit in which a satellite (such as a moon) moves around a planet in the same time that it takes for the planet to make one rotation on its axis.

SYNCHRONOUS ROTATION When two bodies make a complete rotation on their axes in the same time.

As a result, each body always has the same side facing the other. The Moon and Venus are in synchronous rotation with the Earth.

SYNODIC MONTH The complete cycle of phases of the Moon as seen from Earth. It is 29.531 solar days (29 days, 12 hours, 44 minutes, 3 seconds).

SYNODIC PERIOD The time needed for an object within the solar system, such as a planet, to return to the same place relative to the Sun as seen from the Earth.

TANGENT A direction at right angles to a line radiating from a circle or sphere.

If you make a wheel spin, for example, by repeatedly giving it a glancing blow with your hand, the glancing blow is moving along a tangent.

TELECOMMUNICATIONS Sending messages by means of telemetry, using signals made into waves such as radio waves.

THEORY OF RELATIVITY A theory based on how physical laws change when an observer is moving. Its most famous equation says that at the speed of light, energy is related to mass and the speed of light.

THERMOSPHERE A region of the upper atmosphere above the mesosphere.

It absorbs ultraviolet radiation and is where the ionosphere has most effect.

THRUST A very strong and continued pressure.

THRUSTER A term for a small rocket engine.

TIDE Any kind of regular, or cyclic, change that occurs due to the effect of the gravity of one body on another.

We are used to the ocean waters of the Earth being affected by the gravitational pull of the Moon, but tides also cause a small alteration of the shape of a body. This is important in determining the shape of many moons and may even be a source of heating in some.

See also: **NEAP TIDE** and **SPRING TIDE.**

TOPOGRAPHY The shape of the land surface in terms of height.

TOTAL ECLIPSE When one body (such as the Moon or Earth) completely obscures the light source from another body (such as the Earth or Moon).

A total eclipse of the Sun occurs when it is completely blocked out by the Moon.

A total eclipse of the Moon occurs when it passes into the Earth's shadow to such a degree that light from the Sun is completely blocked out.

TRAJECTORY The curved path followed by a projectile.

See also: **SLINGSHOT TRAJECTORY.**

TRANSPONDER Wireless receiver and transmitter.

TROPOSPHERE The lowest region of the atmosphere, where all of the Earth's clouds form.

TRUSS Tubing arrayed in the form of triangles and designed to make a strong frame.

ULTRAVIOLET A form of radiation that is just beyond the violet end of the visible spectrum and so is called "ultra" (more than) violet. At the other end of the visible spectrum is "infra" (less than) red.

UMBRA (1) A region that is in complete darkness during an eclipse.

(2) The darkest region in the center of a sunspot.

UNIVERSE The entirety of everything there is; the cosmos.

Many space scientists prefer to use the term "cosmos," referring to the entirety of energy and matter.

UNSTABLE In atmospheric terms the potential churning of the air in the atmosphere as a result of air being heated from below. There is a chance of the warmed, less-dense air rising through the overlying colder, more-dense air.

UPLINK A communication from Earth to a spacecraft.

URANUS The seventh planet from the Sun and four planets farther from the Sun than the Earth.

Its diameter is four times that of the Earth. It is one of the gas giant planets.

VACUUM A space that is entirely empty.

A vacuum lacks any matter.

VALLEY A natural long depression in the landscape.

VELOCITY A more precise word to describe how something is moving, because movement has both a magnitude (speed) and a direction.

VENT The tube or fissure that allows volcanic materials to reach the surface of a planet.

VENUS The second planet from the Sun and our closest neighbor.

It appears as an evening and morning "star" in the sky. Venus is very similar to the Earth in size and mass.

VOLCANO A mound or mountain that is formed from ash or lava.

VOYAGER A pair of U.S. space probes designed to provide detailed information about the outer regions of the solar system.

Voyager 1 was launched on September 5, 1977. Voyager 2 was launched on August 20, 1977, but traveled more slowly than Voyager 1. Both Voyagers are expected to remain operational until 2020, by which time they will be well outside the solar system.

WATER CYCLE The continuous cycling of water, as vapor, liquid, and solid, between the oceans, the atmosphere, and the land.

WATER VAPOR The gaseous form of water. Also sometimes referred to as moisture.

WEATHERING The breaking down of a rock, perhaps by water, ice, or repeated heating and cooling.

WHITE DWARF Any star originally of low mass that has reached the end of its life.

X-RAY An invisible form of radiation that has extremely short wavelengths just beyond the ultraviolet.

X-rays can go through many materials that light will not.

SET INDEX

Using the set index

This index covers all eight volumes in the *Space Science* set:

Vol. no. Title
1: *How the universe works*
2: *Sun and solar system*
3: *Earth and Moon*
4: *Rocky planets*
5: *Gas giants*
6: *Journey into space*
7: *Shuttle to Space Station*
8: *What satellites see*

An example entry:
Index entries are listed alphabetically.

Moon rover **3:** 48–49, **6:** 51

Volume numbers are in bold and are followed by page references.

In the example above, "Moon rover" appears in Volume 3: *Earth and Moon* on pages 48–49 and in Volume 6: *Journey into space* on page 51. Many terms are also covered separately in the Glossary on pages 58–64.

See, *see also*, or *see under* refers to another entry where there will be additional relevant information.